GCSE English

Jane Eyre

by Charlotte Brontë

Jane Eyre is a classic tale of romance against the odds,
but it's not the easiest book to write GCSE essays about.

Not to worry. This brilliant Text Guide explains the whole thing —
characters, language, themes, historical background... the lot. And because
it's a CGP book, we get straight to the point, with no needless rambling.

We've also included plenty of practice questions to test you on what you've
learned, plus advice on how to plan and write top-grade answers in the exam!
So you can go out in a blaze of glory, just like Mr Rochester almost did.

The Text Guide

CONTENTS

Introduction

Section One — Background and Context

Section Two — Discussion of Chapters

Section Three — Characters

CONTENTS

Section Four — Themes

Section Five — Writer's Techniques

Section Six — Exam Advice

The Characters in 'Jane Eyre'
'Jane Eyre' Cartoon

Published by CGP

Editors:
Lucy Loveluck
Matt Topping
Jennifer Underwood

Contributor:
Elisabeth Quincey

With thanks to Claire Boulter and Nicola Woodfin for the proofreading,
and Jan Greenway for the copyright research.

Acknowledgements:
Cover image and image on page 4 by Lee Avison/Trevillion Images.

Page 16: Illustration by F. H. Townsend, 1868-1920.

With thanks to Alamy for permission to use the images on pages 3, 6, 8, 9, 15, 21, 22, 30, 33, 34, 40, 51, 56 & 59.

With thanks to BBC Photo Library for permission to use the images on pages 3, 4, 5, 13, 14, 17, 19, 26, 35, 38, 39, 43, 48, 54 & 60.

With thanks to iStockphoto.com for permission to use the images on pages 1, 2, 7, 23, 24, 25, 55 & 58.

With thanks to the Kobal Collection for permission to use the images on pages 3, 4, 5, 18, 36, 37 & 46.

With thanks to Mary Evans Picture Library for permission to use the image on page 1.

With thanks to REX Features for permission to use the images on pages 3, 5, 12, 20, 31, 32, 44, 45, 47, 49, 50 & 57.

Every effort has been made to locate copyright holders and obtain permission to reproduce sources.
For those sources where it has been difficult to trace the copyright holder of the work, we would be grateful
for information. If any copyright holder would like us to make an amendment to the acknowledgements,
please notify us and we will gladly update the book at the next reprint. Thank you.

ISBN: 978 1 78294 310 5
Printed by Elanders Ltd, Newcastle upon Tyne.
Clipart from Corel®

Based on the classic CGP style created by Richard Parsons.

Introduction to 'Jane Eyre' and Charlotte Brontë

'Jane Eyre' isn't a typical love story

- *Jane Eyre* is about a lonely <u>orphan</u> who works as a governess and falls in love with her <u>employer</u>.

- Although the novel is <u>fictional</u>, it's based on some of Charlotte Brontë's own <u>experiences</u>.

Women in 19th-Century Britain

1) In the Victorian period, women were considered <u>inferior</u> to men. They were expected to <u>get married</u> and look after the <u>home</u>. Their money belonged to their husband, and they didn't have many <u>rights</u>.

2) <u>Unmarried</u> middle-class women didn't have many options. They could live with <u>relatives</u> or work as <u>teachers</u>.

3) <u>Governesses</u> were live-in teachers for upper-class children. They weren't servants, but they were quite <u>low-status</u> and badly paid.

© iStockphoto.com/ilbusca

Charlotte Brontë had a tragic life

- Charlotte Brontë was a <u>vicar's daughter</u> who lived in <u>Haworth</u>, West Yorkshire, for most of her life. Her <u>mother died</u> when Charlotte was five years old, and <u>two</u> of her <u>sisters died</u> just four years later.

- Her other two sisters, <u>Emily</u> and <u>Anne</u>, were also <u>authors</u> — Emily wrote *Wuthering Heights* and Anne wrote *The Tenant of Wildfell Hall*. They <u>both died</u> whilst Charlotte was in her <u>thirties</u>, as did their brother, <u>Branwell</u>.

- Charlotte and her sisters first published their work using <u>pseudonyms</u> (false names). They felt that readers would <u>disapprove</u> of their novels if they knew they were written by women.

1816	Born in <u>Thornton</u>, West Yorkshire.
1821	Her mother <u>dies</u>.
1824-25	Attends a <u>boarding school</u> at Cowan Bridge with her sisters. Leaves after two of her sisters <u>die</u> of tuberculosis.
1831-32	<u>Studies</u> at Roe Head School.
1835	Returns to Roe Head as a <u>teacher</u>.
1839-41	Works as a governess and <u>rejects</u> two marriage proposals.
1846	Publishes a collection of <u>poems</u> with her <u>sisters</u>.
1847	<u>'Jane Eyre'</u> is published.
1848-49	Her two remaining sisters and her brother <u>die</u>.
1854	<u>Marries</u> Arthur Bell Nicholls, her father's <u>curate</u>.
1855	<u>Dies</u> during pregnancy, aged 38.

© INTERFOTO / Sammlung Rauch / Mary Evans

Background Information

'Jane Eyre' is set in northern England

Here are the <u>key locations</u> in the novel:

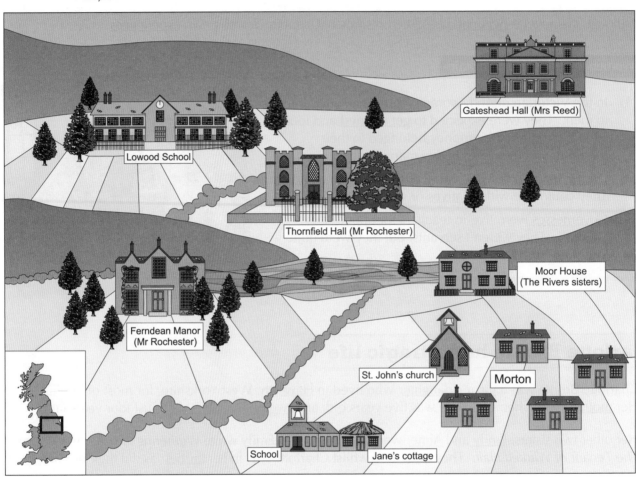

Charlotte Brontë used some of her own experiences

Stanage Edge, Derbyshire — the inspiration for some of the wild scenery in 'Jane Eyre'.

- *Jane Eyre* <u>isn't</u> based on Charlotte Brontë's <u>life</u>, but she used some <u>experiences</u>, <u>places</u> and <u>characters</u> from her own life.

- <u>Lowood school</u> is based on the school at <u>Cowan Bridge</u> where <u>Charlotte</u> was sent aged <u>eight</u>. The overseer of Lowood, <u>Mr Brocklehurst</u>, is based on the person in charge of Cowan Bridge — <u>Reverend Wilson</u>.

- Jane's <u>friend</u> at Lowood, <u>Helen Burns</u>, is based on Charlotte's <u>sister Maria</u>, who <u>died</u> after falling ill at Cowan Bridge.

- Brontë grew up surrounded by the <u>Yorkshire moors</u> and visited the <u>Peak District</u> in Derbyshire. These wild landscapes <u>inspired</u> the setting of <u>Moor House</u> in the novel, and this is where <u>Jane</u> feels at <u>home</u> for the first time in her life.

- Like Jane, Brontë also spent time working as a <u>governess</u> and went back to one of her schools to be a <u>teacher</u>.

Who's Who in 'Jane Eyre'

Jane Eyre...

...is the passionate narrator of the novel. She's a lonely orphan who has her heart broken by her employer, Mr Rochester.

Edward Fairfax Rochester...

...is the eccentric owner of Thornfield Hall. He falls in love with Jane when she comes to work as the governess for his ward, Adèle Varens.

St. John Rivers...

...is a serious, unemotional vicar who turns out to be Jane's cousin.

Bertha Mason...

...is Mr Rochester's first wife. She has gone mad and is secretly kept locked in the attic at Thornfield Hall.

Mary & Diana Rivers...

...are St. John's kind, intelligent sisters. They live at Moor House.

© BBC FILMS/THE KOBAL COLLECTION / SPARHAM, LAURIE

Mrs Fairfax...

...is the welcoming, old-fashioned housekeeper at Thornfield Hall.

Mr Brocklehurst...

...is the cold, cruel man who oversees Lowood School.

Blanche Ingram...

...is a local beauty who everyone thinks is going to marry Mr Rochester.

Mrs Reed...

...is Jane's bitter, widowed aunt at Gateshead. Jane lives with her as a child, which they both hate.

Mr Mason...

...is Bertha's brother, who twice turns up unexpectedly at Thornfield.

Introduction

'Jane Eyre' — Plot Summary

© Lee Avison/Trevillion Images

'Jane Eyre'… what happens when?

Here's a little recap of the <u>main events</u> of *Jane Eyre*. It's a good idea to learn <u>what happens when</u>, so that you know exactly how the <u>plot progresses</u> and how all the important events <u>fit together</u>.

Volume One — Jane goes from Gateshead to Thornfield, via Lowood

© 20TH CENTURY FOX / THE KOBAL COLLECTION

- Jane is a ten-year-old <u>orphan</u> who lives at <u>Gateshead</u> with her rich <u>aunt</u> and <u>cousins</u> — they all <u>dislike</u> Jane.

- Jane gets into a <u>fight</u> with her cousin, <u>John Reed</u>. <u>Mrs Reed</u> locks Jane in the <u>red-room</u>, and Jane falls ill. An <u>apothecary</u> (pharmacist) recommends sending Jane away to <u>school</u>.

- Jane is sent to <u>Lowood</u> school, overseen by the miserly <u>Mr Brocklehurst</u>, but run by the kind <u>Miss Temple</u>. Mr Brocklehurst tells the school that Jane is a <u>liar</u>, but Miss Temple proves her <u>innocence</u>.

- Jane becomes friends with <u>Helen Burns</u>, who later <u>dies</u> of <u>consumption</u> (tuberculosis).

- Eight years later, Jane is now a <u>teacher</u> at <u>Lowood</u> and <u>Miss Temple</u> has left to get <u>married</u>. Jane decides it's time to move on, and <u>advertises</u> as a <u>governess</u> in the local paper.

- <u>Mrs Fairfax</u>, the housekeeper of <u>Thornfield Hall</u>, hires Jane as a <u>governess</u> for a French girl, <u>Adèle Varens</u>. Adèle is the responsibility of <u>Mr Rochester</u>, who owns Thornfield but is <u>away</u> from home.

- Whilst out walking, Jane <u>helps</u> a man who's fallen off his <u>horse</u> — it turns out to be <u>Mr Rochester</u>, who has come <u>home</u>. They start to get to know each other, but Rochester is <u>moody</u> and <u>unpredictable</u>.

- One night, Jane <u>hears</u> a <u>strange</u> noise outside her <u>bedroom</u> door. She discovers that <u>Rochester's bed</u> is on <u>fire</u>. She <u>saves</u> Rochester, who blames the servant <u>Grace Poole</u> for the fire.

Volume Two — A wedding that doesn't work out

- Some of <u>Rochester's friends</u> arrive to stay at <u>Thornfield</u>, including the <u>beautiful Blanche Ingram</u>. Everyone <u>expects</u> that Rochester will <u>marry</u> her.

- <u>Jane</u> has <u>fallen in love</u> with <u>Rochester</u> and believes that she could make him <u>happier</u> than Blanche could.

- Rochester disguises himself as a <u>fortune-teller</u> and tells Blanche that Rochester isn't as rich as she believes. He also <u>tries</u> to get <u>Jane</u> to <u>admit</u> she loves <u>him</u>.

Copyright © BBC Photo Library

- Jane tells Rochester about an <u>unexpected</u> visitor, <u>Mr Mason</u>, who's arrived at Thornfield. Rochester goes <u>pale</u> at the mention of Mr Mason's name, but doesn't reveal why.

- That night, there's a <u>scream</u> from the <u>third floor</u>. Rochester takes Jane to <u>help Mr Mason</u> who's been <u>attacked</u>.

- Jane is summoned to <u>Gateshead</u> to see the dying <u>Mrs Reed</u>. Jane <u>apologises</u> for her behaviour as a child, but Mrs Reed remains <u>bitter</u> towards her.

- Mrs Reed gives Jane an <u>old letter</u> from an <u>uncle</u> Jane didn't know existed. The uncle wanted to <u>adopt</u> Jane, but Mrs Reed told him that Jane was <u>dead</u>.

- Jane returns to <u>Thornfield</u>, and Mr Rochester <u>proposes</u> to her. Two nights before the <u>wedding</u>, Jane is woken by someone coming into her room and <u>tearing</u> her bridal <u>veil</u> in <u>two</u>.

- <u>Mr Mason</u> stops the wedding, saying that Mr Rochester is <u>already married</u> to <u>Bertha Mason</u>. Jane's taken to see Bertha in the <u>attic</u> — she's behind the <u>strange events</u> at Thornfield.

Volume Three — Jane and Mr Rochester eventually marry

- Rochester explains that his family <u>persuaded</u> him to marry Bertha, but then she went <u>mad</u>. He wants Jane to be his <u>mistress</u> because he <u>can't marry</u> her. Jane decides she <u>can't</u> do this, and <u>runs away</u>.

- She <u>nearly dies</u>, but finds her way to <u>Moor House</u> (also known as <u>Marsh End</u>), where she's taken in by the <u>Rivers family</u>, who help her <u>recover</u>.

- Mary and Diana Rivers leave to be <u>governesses</u>, and <u>St. John</u> asks Jane to be a <u>teacher</u> in the local school. She <u>accepts</u> and moves into her <u>own cottage</u> next to the school.

- Jane finds out that the Rivers siblings are her <u>cousins</u>, and their <u>uncle</u> (the one mentioned by Mrs Reed) has <u>died</u> and left Jane a lot of <u>money</u>, which she <u>shares</u> with them.

- St. John is going to <u>India</u> as a <u>missionary</u>, and he asks Jane to go with him as his <u>wife</u>. She <u>refuses</u> to marry him, and he won't take her to India unless she does.

- Jane mysteriously hears <u>Rochester's voice</u> calling her, which persuades her to return to <u>Thornfield</u>. When she gets there, she finds that it's been <u>burnt down</u> by <u>Bertha</u>, who then committed <u>suicide</u>. Rochester <u>tried</u> to <u>save</u> her, but couldn't, and was <u>blinded</u> and <u>injured</u> by the fire.

- Jane tracks down <u>Rochester</u>, who's living at Ferndean Manor. They get <u>married</u>.

- <u>Ten years later</u>, Rochester has <u>regained</u> sight in <u>one eye</u>, and they have a <u>son</u>.

- The novel <u>ends</u> with news of <u>St. John</u>, who is in <u>India</u>, but is likely to <u>die soon</u>.

Jane and Rochester are blinded by love...

... well, and a fire in Rochester's case. Right then, hopefully you've got a decent idea about what actually happens in *Jane Eyre*. There are loads of different characters and locations in the novel, so make sure you've got your head around all the different people and places before you crack on with the rest of the book.

Introduction

Life in Early 19th-Century Britain

Jane Eyre is set about 200 years ago, so life in the novel is pretty different to life as we know it.

England was a rural society

1) *Jane Eyre* is set around the 1820s to 1830s, when England was a <u>rural society</u> — most people lived in the <u>countryside</u> (rather than in towns or cities). This was starting to change, though.

2) Society was <u>divided</u> between the <u>very rich</u> upper classes and the <u>poor working classes</u>.

3) Land and money were controlled by a <u>few</u> rich, powerful <u>families</u> and passed down through <u>inheritance</u>, so it wasn't easy for people from <u>lower</u> social classes to become <u>wealthy</u>.

4) In the novel, Mr Rochester <u>owns lots of land</u>, which he inherited from his family — "Almost all the land... has belonged to the Rochesters time out of mind."

The Industrial Revolution brought change

A mill in Sheffield in the 19th century.

© Classic Image/Alamy

1) The novel is set during the <u>Industrial Revolution</u>.

2) At this time, machines for <u>manufacturing</u> improved and so did transport — this meant that <u>businesses</u> could <u>make</u> their products <u>quickly</u> and <u>cheaply</u> and easily <u>move</u> them around the country.

3) In the early 1800s, hundreds of thousands of people <u>moved</u> to urban areas to <u>work in factories</u>.

4) During the Industrial Revolution it became easier for people to <u>get rich</u> by investing in <u>industry</u> (like Rosamond Oliver's family, who own a needle factory). People who earned lots of money this way could <u>socialise</u> with the upper classes, but they had a <u>lower status</u> than people who had inherited their wealth.

Britain had links with many foreign countries

1) By the early 19th century, Britain <u>ruled</u> a lot of other countries, which formed the <u>British Empire</u>. This made it <u>rich</u> and <u>powerful</u>.

2) Foreign trade also provided <u>new business opportunities</u> — Jane's uncle, <u>John Eyre</u>, made his fortune trading in <u>Madeira</u>.

3) Some British people also travelled abroad as <u>missionaries</u> — they wanted to <u>convert</u> people to Christianity. In the novel, <u>St. John</u> leaves for India to work as a missionary.

4) <u>Racial prejudices</u> were common in 19th-century society — there are hints in the novel that Bertha Mason, Mr Rochester's Creole (and possibly mixed-race) wife, is seen as <u>inferior</u> because of her <u>race</u>.

> **Theme — Foreignness**
>
> You never know exactly what goes on when characters in *Jane Eyre* are <u>abroad</u> — there's an air of <u>mystery</u> around them. Mr Rochester tells Jane that he made a "<u>capital error</u>" while in the Caribbean, but at first he keeps the details a <u>secret</u>.

"he realised a fortune of twenty thousand pounds."

John Eyre was Jane and the Rivers' uncle — he invested in risky new businesses abroad and got rich. Jane never meets him, and doesn't know he exists for most of the novel, but inherits his large fortune — winner.

Life in Early 19th-Century Britain

You might not always appreciate it, but getting an education is easy these days — no such luck back then...

Not everybody went to school

1) *Jane Eyre* is set in a time when <u>education</u> was a <u>privilege</u>. <u>Wealthy</u> families could afford to send their children away to school, or to hire a <u>governess</u> to come and live with them and teach the children.

2) School was not compulsory, and the <u>government</u> only began <u>funding</u> schools in 1833.

3) Many schools were run by the <u>Church</u> — Lowood school is run by Mr Brocklehurst, a clergyman, and supported by charity <u>donations</u>.

Young girls in a 19th century classroom.

Theme — Gender

<u>Education</u> is Jane's route to <u>autonomy</u> and freedom. She doesn't have to depend on her family or on a husband for money because she can <u>teach</u>.

4) <u>Boys</u>' education was more of a priority — St. John Rivers has already established a school for boys at <u>Morton</u>, but asks Jane to teach at a new school for girls. This school is funded by <u>Miss Oliver</u> — a wealthy local lady.

5) At this time, <u>women</u> couldn't go to <u>university</u>.

6) The <u>Rivers sisters</u> are women who value and enjoy <u>learning</u>. The fact that Brontë presents them as such likeable, well-rounded characters suggests that she believes in the <u>importance</u> of <u>education</u> for <u>women</u>.

Many people suffered with disease

1) People often <u>died young</u> in the 19th century, because <u>medical resources</u> and sanitation were less advanced — when Jane falls ill at Gateshead, the servants wonder if she will die.

2) Infectious diseases such as <u>typhus</u>, <u>typhoid</u> and <u>tuberculosis (TB)</u> were quite common in the early 19th century. They were often <u>fatal</u>.

3) <u>Charlotte Brontë</u> survived a typhoid outbreak in her first year of school at Cowan Bridge, but two of her sisters died of <u>TB</u> just months later.

Character — Helen Burns

Helen Burns is based on <u>Maria Brontë</u> — Charlotte's sister who <u>died</u> of <u>TB</u>. Charlotte Brontë also uses her <u>experience</u> of <u>disease</u> at Cowan Bridge in the novel — many Lowood pupils die of <u>typhus</u>.

Mental illness wasn't very well-understood

1) In the early nineteenth century, people didn't <u>know</u> a lot about <u>mental illness</u>, and they didn't really have any way to <u>treat</u> it effectively.

2) People usually tried to <u>separate</u> the mentally ill from the rest of society — just like Mr Rochester locks <u>Bertha</u> away.

3) If they could <u>afford</u> it, some people cared for mentally ill relatives at <u>home</u>. Otherwise, they sent them to <u>lunatic asylums</u>, where they were often badly treated.

EXAM TIP

Remember that life was very different in the 19th century...

The examiner will be dead impressed if you can link a point to the time in which *Jane Eyre* is set. There's no point thinking of the novel as if it was taking place today — things would turn out completely differently.

Section One — Background and Context

Women in Early 19th-Century Society

Women were usually dependent on men and had fewer rights — but Jane's relatively independent at the point at which she marries Mr Rochester.

Women were often dependent on men

1) During the early 19th century, women were normally dependent on the men in their family, especially in the upper classes. It was usually men who earned a living or owned land which generated income from rent.

2) Women didn't have the vote, and generally had to do what their husband told them — Jane fears the power that St. John would have over her if they got married.

3) There are several examples in the novel of women being dependent on men:

- The Reed women get into financial trouble because John Reed inherited (and spent) the family fortune — his mother and sisters don't have much money themselves.

- At Thornfield, Mrs Fairfax, Adèle, Jane and Bertha are all financially dependent on Mr Rochester.

- All of the pupils and staff at Lowood school depend on Mr Brocklehurst, and they suffer because of it. Although Miss Temple shows some independence by giving the girls extra food, Mr Brocklehurst criticises her for it.

4) There weren't many 'respectable' job options for single women who belonged to the upper middle classes — they could work as governesses, like Jane and the Rivers sisters, but that's about it.

Marrying a rich man gave women financial security

© Moviestore Collection/Alamy

1) A woman's best chance of a stable financial future was a good marriage. This is why Blanche Ingram is so keen to marry Mr Rochester (until she believes he's not that rich) and Georgiana Reed marries a rich older man who will support her.

2) Many women didn't have financial assets to attract a husband, so they needed to be pretty and have a good reputation.

3) Women often weren't taught to read or write. Instead they learnt skills that would attract a husband, such as singing or dancing.

4) Marriage was also a way to progress in society — when Miss Temple marries, she can leave Lowood.

Jane becomes independent

1) It was almost impossible for women at that time to be independent of men. They couldn't vote and had few rights. But Charlotte Brontë valued women with independent spirits, like Jane.

2) When Jane starts teaching at Morton village school, she lives independently for the first time. This was a rare situation for women in the early nineteenth century.

KEY QUOTE *"I am a free human being with an independent will"*

Jane lives in a time when women are usually dependent on men, but she doesn't let that stop her. She's determined to be her own person — at the end of the novel she's emotionally and financially independent.

Social Classes in the Early 19th Century

Society was split into lots of different classes — you were expected to know your place, and stay there.

There were big divisions within the upper classes

1) The highest level of the upper classes didn't need to work because they earned money from renting out their land, which they'd inherited. Mr Rochester is in this situation.

2) The next level down were rich people who had earned their money through a trade or profession. e.g. Rosamond Oliver's father.

3) People who earned money from a profession or from trade were looked down on by people who didn't need to work. In the novel, Mrs Reed looks down on Jane's uncle because he's made his money through trade.

4) Members of the clergy were usually respected whether they were rich or poor. In the novel Mr Brocklehurst is a rich clergyman, but St. John Rivers is relatively poor. However, Jane's father was a poor clergyman who the Reed family disapproved of.

> Charlotte Brontë criticises the divisions in society — many of the upper-class characters in *Jane Eyre* are not very nice people, for example Mrs Reed, Mr Brocklehurst and Miss Ingram.

Many people were dependent on the upper classes

1) Servants and other working-class people relied on wealthy employers to pay them so they could live. Bessie is a servant at Gateshead, so she must obey Mrs Reed, who is her employer.

2) Jane is "less than a servant" when she's living with the Reeds — she's an extra dependant that they'd rather not have. She is then dependent on society while living as a charity student at Lowood.

Governesses didn't really fit into any social class

Brontë worked as a governess, so she experienced this lack of belonging first-hand.

1) Governesses had the manners and education of the upper classes, so they could teach them to their pupils. They usually had little money and weren't considered as equals by members of the upper classes. But they weren't really servants, either.

2) Jane doesn't really belong in any part of society. Her education has helped make her an equal match for Mr Rochester, but in terms of class, they are not equal at all. Mrs Fairfax is shocked by their marriage because it's not the done thing.

3) Mr Rochester's friends ignore Jane. Blanche Ingram openly discusses her snobbish dislike of governesses.

4) The fact that Jane is well-spoken and well-dressed causes problems when she asks for help at the bakery in Morton — working-class people are suspicious of her.

© AF archive/Alamy

Theme — Love and Marriage

The romance between Jane and Mr Rochester challenges social conventions, even though she only marries him when she's got her own money — this handily makes it socially acceptable.

KEY QUOTE

"because I am poor... I am soulless and heartless?"

Jane gets peeved when Mr Rochester suggests she has no feelings for him, but she doesn't actually believe he's saying that poor people have no soul. Unlike most people, he doesn't really care about social class.

Practice Questions

And that's the end of Section One. To help make sure you've got it all sorted, here's a page of lovely questions for you. They're just to check you've been paying attention, so you only need to write a few words for each one.

Quick Questions

1) How did the Industrial Revolution help people to get rich?

2) Name three foreign places that characters in *Jane Eyre* visit.

3) What was the role of a governess in the 19th century?

4) Why didn't all children attend school in the 19th century?

5) Name two schools that feature in *Jane Eyre*.

6) Name two infectious diseases that were common in the early 19th century?

7) Which of the following statements about women in the early 19th century is NOT true?
   a) They were often dependent on men.
   b) It was considered important for women to be as educated as men.
   c) They had few rights.

8) Who looked down on people who made their money through trade in the 19th century?

Practice Questions

Now for some questions that might require a bit more brainpower. Being able to bring in some of the novel's background and context will really add something to your exam answers, so put some effort into these questions.

In-depth Questions

1) What evidence is there in the experiences of the Brontë family and the story of *Jane Eyre* that schools in the early 19th century weren't very healthy places?

2) Women in early 19th-century society often had to marry to find financial security. How does Charlotte Brontë emphasise this in the novel?

3) How does Charlotte Brontë use the characters in *Jane Eyre* to criticise the divisions in Victorian society? Use quotes from the text to support your answer.

4) Why didn't governesses really fit into any of the social classes? What evidence of this is there in *Jane Eyre*?

Volume One — Chapters 1-4

By now, hopefully you've had a look at the social context and got your head around the plot. This section explores the novel in much more detail — analysing its key events.

Jane is treated unjustly as a child at Gateshead

Jane is aged 10 here, but she is narrating the novel aged about 30, so she's got the benefit of hindsight.

1) Jane lives with her <u>aunt</u> and her three children, <u>Eliza</u>, <u>Georgiana</u> and <u>John</u>, who all <u>dislike</u> her.

2) She is treated <u>brutally</u> by John. Her aunt is also <u>cruel</u> to her — she shuts Jane in the "<u>red-room</u>" as a punishment for <u>fighting</u> with <u>John</u>. Jane thinks the room is haunted — she's <u>terrified</u> and falls <u>ill</u> after the incident.

Theme — Family

Jane is an <u>orphan</u> — after both her parents died, she was taken in by her <u>Uncle Reed</u>. He also died, leaving Jane to be looked after <u>reluctantly</u> by <u>Aunt Reed</u>. Jane thinks she has <u>no</u> other <u>relations</u>, or if she does, they are "poor, low relations".

3) After Jane's <u>mistreatment</u> and <u>illness</u>, an apothecary (pharmacist) called <u>Mr Lloyd</u> listens kindly to her story.

4) He <u>recommends</u> that Jane should go away to <u>school</u> — she's keen to <u>get away</u> from Gateshead.

Theme — Outsiders

Jane has <u>no one</u> on her side at Gateshead and knows she <u>doesn't fit</u> in — "I was like nobody there". She's <u>badly treated</u> by her relations, and doesn't belong with the <u>servants</u>. Although one maid, <u>Bessie</u>, is <u>kind</u> to Jane <u>sometimes</u>, she has a "hasty temper".

Mrs Reed is shocked by Jane's passionate outburst

1) Aunt Reed introduces Jane to <u>Mr Brocklehurst</u>, who owns the <u>school</u> she will go to (Lowood).

2) She tells Mr Brocklehurst about Jane's <u>wicked ways</u> and <u>deceitful nature</u>, which <u>upsets Jane</u>.

3) After Mr Brocklehurst has gone, Jane speaks very <u>bluntly</u> and <u>passionately</u> to her aunt, telling her, "I will <u>never</u> call you <u>aunt</u> again" and reminds her aunt how <u>badly</u> she has treated her.

4) Jane is telling the <u>truth</u>, but her aunt is <u>shocked</u> and troubled by the outburst. You can see Jane <u>developing</u> as a character here — she <u>stands up</u> to Mrs Reed.

© Moviestore/REX

Character — Mrs Reed

Although the <u>way</u> that Jane <u>speaks</u> to her aunt is disrespectful, Brontë describes so much of Jane's <u>mistreatment</u> that the reader <u>sympathises</u> with her. Aunt Reed "looked frightened" when Jane accused her of being "<u>deceitful</u>", suggesting that she knows that she is <u>hypocritical</u> and not a good Christian herself. This is confirmed later on when Aunt Reed withholds information about Jane's Uncle.

KEY QUOTE *"Did ever anybody see such a picture of passion!"*

Jane's passion and emotions are key aspects of her character, even as a child. In the 19th century, being a passionate woman was a big no-no, so Jane's strong emotions often take people by surprise. You go, girl!

Volume One — Chapters 5-7

At first, Jane's pleased about being sent to school — but it doesn't turn out too well...

Jane leaves Gateshead for Lowood School

1) Jane travels <u>alone</u> to Lowood, and the teachers think that she is "<u>very young</u>" to travel <u>so far</u> on her own — she already seems <u>isolated</u>.

2) The conditions at the school are <u>dreadful</u>. The girls at Lowood don't have much <u>food</u>, and the place is <u>freezing cold</u> in winter.

3) <u>Miss Temple</u> is a teacher who is <u>kind</u> to Jane and the rest of the girls. She does what she can to <u>improve</u> the conditions, but she is restricted by the <u>stingy Mr Brocklehurst</u>.

Copyright © BBC Photo Library

4) Jane spends a lot of these chapters <u>observing</u> and <u>commenting</u> on the school's <u>routines</u> and <u>rules</u>. Brontë seems to be <u>criticising</u> real-life schools like Lowood, where children were <u>treated</u> so <u>badly</u>.

Jane meets Helen Burns

1) <u>Helen Burns</u> is another <u>pupil</u> at Lowood. She is <u>often punished</u> by a teacher, Miss Scatcherd.

2) Jane asks Helen lots of <u>questions</u>, and can't <u>understand</u> how she <u>puts up</u> with Miss Scatcherd's "cross and cruel" actions.

3) Jane tells Helen her own <u>story</u>, and Helen says that although her aunt has treated her <u>unkindly</u>, she should try to <u>forgive</u> her. Because of her <u>Christian faith</u>, Helen believes that the teachers are right to <u>punish</u> her, and she tells Jane that it's important to "<u>Love your enemies</u>".

For more about religion in the novel, see p.45.

4) Helen offers Jane an <u>alternative point of view</u> — that life is too short to be "nursing animosity" and "registering wrongs" — but Jane <u>doesn't</u> really <u>take it in</u>.

Mr Brocklehurst visits the school

Character — Mr Brocklehurst

Brontë presents Mr Brocklehurst as a <u>cruel</u> and <u>hypocritcal</u> character. He's a clergyman with a <u>harsh</u> interpretation of <u>Christianity</u>. His <u>miserly</u> treatment of the girls at Lowood <u>contrasts</u> with his own <u>lavishly</u> dressed wife and daughters.

1) Mr Brocklehurst <u>visits Lowood</u> three weeks after Jane's arrival. He is <u>critical</u> of Miss Temple and insists that any girl with <u>long hair</u> must have it <u>cut</u> off. Miss Temple seems to <u>disagree</u> with Mr Brocklehurst, but she is <u>powerless</u> compared to him.

2) Jane's been <u>dreading</u> Mr Brocklehurst's visit because <u>Mrs Reed</u> had told him she was "deceitful". When he notices Jane, he makes her stand on a <u>stool</u> and tells the <u>whole school</u> that she's "<u>a liar</u>" and that they should "avoid her company".

3) Jane thinks that the <u>pupils</u> and <u>teachers</u> will <u>turn against</u> her, but Helen passes her and gives her a "smile" which helps her <u>endure</u> the punishment.

Link 'Jane Eyre' to Brontë's life...

Brontë went to a boarding school, and blamed her sisters' deaths on the poor conditions there. Jane's descriptions expose the terrible conditions in schools at the time. It'd put me off going, that's for sure.

Volume One — Chapters 8-9

Eight chapters in, and life is finally starting to look a bit brighter for poor little Jane.

Helen and Jane become friends

1) Helen Burns <u>comforts</u> Jane after she is "<u>crushed</u>" by Mr Brocklehurst, and <u>tells</u> her that he's "<u>little liked</u>" by the girls and teachers. Helen teaches Jane about religion and morality — she should trust her "<u>own conscience</u>" rather than the opinions of others.

> **Theme — Morality**
>
> Miss Temple believes in <u>justice</u> — she refuses to <u>blindly accept</u> the accusations against Jane and <u>actively</u> seeks the <u>truth</u> for herself.

2) <u>Miss Temple</u> listens to Jane's story about her life. Jane is much more "<u>restrained</u>" than when she told the story to Helen — she's <u>learnt</u> from Helen and is becoming more <u>mature</u>.

3) Jane finds listening to Miss Temple and Helen's <u>conversation</u> a "privilege" and wants to be <u>like them</u>. It becomes <u>obvious</u> to the reader that Helen is <u>seriously ill</u>, but <u>Jane</u> appears <u>unaware</u> of it.

4) Miss Temple writes to <u>Mr Lloyd</u>, the apothecary who <u>helped</u> Jane at Gateshead, to see if he <u>agrees</u> with Jane's story of her <u>mistreatment</u>. Jane is very <u>relieved</u> when Mr Lloyd writes back and <u>confirms</u> what she said, and when Miss Temple publicly <u>clears her</u> of being a liar.

Spring comes to Lowood... but so does illness

1) <u>Spring</u> arrives, but <u>many girls</u> fall ill with <u>typhus</u>. Jane claims that these illnesses are because of "<u>semi-starvation</u> and neglected <u>colds</u>".

> **Writer's Techniques**
>
> Brontë uses the <u>changing seasons</u> to symbolise the <u>changes</u> in <u>Jane's mood</u>. Just as the "<u>frosts</u> of winter" are replaced by the <u>warmth</u> of spring, Jane <u>enjoys</u> life more, and her <u>unhappiness</u> at <u>Gateshead</u> is replaced by <u>freedom</u> at <u>Lowood</u>.

2) Some of the girls <u>die</u>. Jane, and the others who remain well, get much more <u>freedom</u> and there's <u>more food</u> to go around.

3) Helen Burns is <u>ill</u> in bed, so Jane becomes friendly with <u>Mary Ann Wilson</u> — a girl who <u>contrasts</u> with Helen because she <u>doesn't improve</u> Jane.

Helen Burns dies

Copyright © BBC Photo Library

1) Jane thinks that because <u>Helen</u> has <u>consumption</u> (tuberculosis) rather than typhus, it's "mild" and she will get <u>better</u>. This emphasises her naivety.

2) <u>Readers</u> of the novel know that <u>consumption</u> was <u>fatal</u> at the time. When Jane sees the <u>surgeon</u> she realises that Helen must be <u>very ill</u>. A nurse tells her that Helen is likely to <u>die</u> very <u>soon</u>.

3) Jane is <u>upset</u>, and creeps to Miss Temple's room, where <u>Helen</u> is, to "give her one last kiss".

4) She gets into Helen's bed, where Helen tells Jane that she is <u>not frightened</u> of dying and that her <u>mind</u> is at <u>rest</u>. They go to <u>sleep</u>, and Helen <u>dies</u> during the night.

KEY QUOTE

"I believe; I have faith: I am going to God."

Helen Burns dies peacefully, believing that she is going to heaven and will "escape great sufferings" by dying young. She spends her last waking minutes answering Jane's questions and reassuring her about God.

Section Two — Discussion of Chapters

Volume One — Chapters 10-11

There are often some boring years in a person's life, but Brontë doesn't bother telling you about them.

The novel mostly skips the next eight years

Jane's control as the narrator is shown here — she decides that her adolescent years aren't worth hearing about. See p.54-55.

1) Jane is now <u>eighteen</u> and works as a <u>teacher</u> at <u>Lowood</u>.

2) After the <u>typhus</u> outbreak, <u>people</u> found out how <u>bad</u> the conditions at the school were, and stepped in to <u>improve</u> things. <u>Mr Brocklehurst</u> was exposed as <u>uncaring</u> and <u>stingy</u>.

Theme — The Supernatural

Jane describes the <u>idea</u> of advertising for work as if "A kind <u>fairy</u> ... dropped the required suggestion on my pillow". This could suggest something <u>supernatural</u> happened to <u>help</u> her.

3) Jane says that she got an "<u>excellent education</u>" and that the school had "<u>value and importance</u>". This suggests that Brontë is emphasising how important education is.

4) When <u>Miss Temple</u> gets <u>married</u> and <u>leaves</u> the school, <u>Jane</u> decides that she wants "<u>liberty</u>". She knows that she can't be <u>truly free</u>, because she is poor, but she looks for a "new servitude" and <u>advertises</u> for work as a <u>governess</u>. She receives one reply — from <u>Mrs Fairfax</u> at <u>Thornfield Hall</u>.

5) Jane is about to leave Lowood when <u>Bessie</u> arrives. She tells Jane that the <u>Reeds</u> are <u>unhappy</u> and <u>struggling financially</u>. Bessie also mentions an <u>uncle</u> from <u>Madeira</u> who came looking for Jane seven years ago. This is Brontë's first <u>hint</u> that Jane has another <u>family member</u> who could become <u>important</u>.

Jane arrives at Thornfield

Jane's 'home' changes for the first time in eight years — this is a big move for her.

1) Jane is welcomed <u>kindly</u> by Mrs Fairfax, whose room has a "<u>cheerful fire</u>" — this is a <u>big contrast</u> to Lowood.

2) Jane is going to be the <u>governess</u> of a young <u>French</u> girl, <u>Adèle Varens</u>.

3) Jane assumes that Mrs Fairfax is the <u>lady</u> of the house, but is <u>relieved</u> when she finds out that she is only the <u>housekeeper</u> as it means that they are more <u>equal</u>.

4) <u>Mr Rochester</u>, the owner of Thornfield, is <u>absent</u> when Jane arrives. He is described by Mrs Fairfax as being "<u>just</u> and <u>liberal</u>" but "rather <u>peculiar</u>".

5) Mrs Fairfax shows Jane around, and Jane hears a <u>strange laugh</u>, just after describing part of Thornfield as being like "<u>Bluebeard's castle</u>". Mrs Fairfax blames the laughter on a servant, <u>Grace Poole</u>.

Theme — Secrecy and Deception

<u>Bluebeard</u> is a <u>folk tale character</u> who allows his <u>wife</u> to enter <u>any room</u> in his castle <u>except one</u>. She <u>disobeys</u> the order, and finds the <u>dead bodies</u> of Bluebeard's <u>previous wives</u> inside the forbidden room. This <u>foreshadows</u> later events in the novel, when it turns out Mr Rochester has <u>locked</u> his <u>first wife</u> away upstairs.

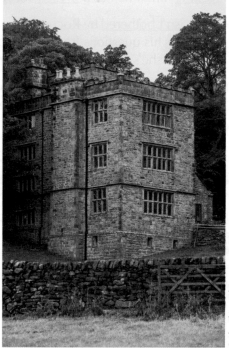

© Alex Ekins / Alamy

Mention fire as an important symbol...

The warm fire in Mrs Fairfax's room is welcoming in contrast to frosty Lowood. Fire is used as a motif throughout the novel — it can suggest warmth and passion, but also represent danger...

Volume One — Chapters 12-15

Jane quickly gets to grips with her new work as a governess, but life is about to change...

Jane's quiet life is disturbed by the arrival of Mr Rochester

© Illustration by F. H. Townsend, 1868-1920

1) Jane is reasonably <u>content</u> with life at Thornfield, but it's all a bit <u>dull</u>, and she's <u>frustrated</u> by how women are expected to "<u>confine</u> themselves" to a boring life.

2) One evening whilst out <u>walking</u>, she hears a sound on the road. She thinks it might be a "<u>Gytrash</u>" — a <u>supernatural</u> black <u>dog</u> or <u>horse</u>. It turns out to be a man riding a horse, and his dog.

3) The <u>horse slips</u> on the ice and its <u>rider falls off</u>. Jane <u>helps</u> the man, but he <u>doesn't</u> reveal his <u>identity</u> to her.

4) Jane doesn't really want to <u>return</u> to Thornfield and describes her life there as "<u>stagnation</u>". However, back at the house, she sees the man's <u>dog</u> and <u>discovers</u> that the man she helped was <u>Mr Rochester</u>.

Character — Jane

Jane meets Mr Rochester <u>without</u> realising <u>who</u> he is — she's <u>not afraid</u> of him and <u>helps</u> him, and this <u>foreshadows</u> their later, successful <u>relationship</u>. Key moments in their relationship are often when Jane is <u>helping</u> him.

Mr Rochester interrogates Jane

1) <u>Adèle</u> is <u>excited</u> to see Mr Rochester and keeps <u>asking</u> him if he has a <u>present</u> for her.

2) Jane <u>isn't bothered</u> by Rochester's <u>abrupt</u> manner and <u>answers</u> his questions <u>frankly</u>. He <u>criticises Jane</u> and tells her she's <u>different</u> from other young <u>governesses</u>.

Character — Adèle

Rochester tells Jane that <u>Adèle</u> is the <u>illegitimate daughter</u> of a <u>French opera star</u> — Céline Varens. He had a <u>love affair</u> with Céline, but he says Adèle <u>isn't</u> his <u>daughter</u>. Jane feels more <u>sympathetic</u> to Adèle now she knows she is a "<u>lonely little orphan</u>".

3) <u>Rochester</u> tells Jane that at some point in her <u>life</u> she will <u>experience</u> a "<u>craggy pass</u> in the channel", where <u>falling in love</u> will <u>disrupt</u> her life — this seems to <u>predict</u> Jane's <u>future</u> with him.

4) Rochester also <u>admits</u> to some <u>past mistakes</u> — it <u>seems</u> as if he and Jane can be <u>honest</u> with <u>each other</u>.

Jane saves Mr Rochester from a fire

1) One night, Jane <u>hears</u> a "<u>demoniac laugh</u>" outside her <u>room</u> — she <u>suspects</u> the <u>mysterious Grace Poole</u>.

Character — Grace Poole

Grace is a <u>servant</u> at <u>Thornfield</u>, who is <u>blamed</u> for the <u>strange noises</u> and the <u>fire</u>. <u>Jane</u> wonders if she's "<u>possessed</u> with a <u>devil</u>" — she's presented as a <u>mysterious</u>, <u>threatening</u> character.

2) Jane sees <u>smoke</u> coming from <u>Rochester's room</u> and rushes in to <u>wake</u> him up. His <u>bed</u> is on <u>fire</u>, but Jane manages to <u>put out</u> the <u>flames</u>. Rochester <u>thanks</u> Jane, and seems to be <u>full</u> of <u>unspoken words</u> as she goes back to bed. He doesn't want her to <u>leave</u>, and there's the first <u>hint</u> of a <u>romantic connection</u> between the two of them.

3) Volume One ends on a bit of a <u>cliffhanger</u> — <u>who</u> started the <u>fire</u>, and is Jane <u>safe</u> at Thornfield?

"Strange energy was in his voice, strange fire in his look..."

Nothing brings people closer than a good old damsel in distress scenario. Although it's Mr Rochester who's in distress, and Jane who comes to the rescue. Nobody declares anything, but there's something brewing.

Volume Two — Chapters 1-2 (16-17*)

If you thought that the fire might bring Jane and Mr Rochester together, I'm afraid you were wrong...

Jane goes through a period of mental turmoil

1) After the <u>fire</u>, Jane feels <u>nervous</u> about seeing Mr Rochester again, but she also <u>wants</u> to see him. However, he's <u>gone</u> to visit a local family, and Mrs Fairfax suggests he's socialising with some "<u>beautiful women</u>".

2) Jane has <u>feelings</u> for Rochester, but she knows that she's <u>lower status</u> than the ladies that Rochester is <u>socialising</u> with.

3) She <u>forces</u> her feelings into a "course of wholesome <u>discipline</u>" and paints an <u>imagined portrait</u> of the beautiful <u>Blanche Ingram</u> (one of the young ladies) to compare with a "poor, and plain" <u>self-portrait</u>.

4) When Jane hears that Mr Rochester is <u>coming back</u>, she <u>spills</u> her <u>coffee</u>, with <u>nerves</u> or <u>excitement</u>.

> **Theme — Secrecy and Deception**
>
> Jane <u>overhears</u> two <u>servants</u> talking about <u>Grace</u>. They say she gets "good wages" and does a <u>job</u> that <u>most</u> people <u>couldn't do</u>. They <u>stop</u> talking when they notice <u>Jane</u>, and Jane is <u>excluded</u> from the <u>secret</u>.

Blanche Ingram arrives at Thornfield

1) <u>Mr Rochester</u> returns to <u>Thornfield</u>, accompanied by <u>Blanche Ingram</u> and some other <u>upper-class guests</u>.

2) Jane <u>tries</u> to stay <u>out</u> of the <u>way</u>, but Mr Rochester <u>makes</u> her come to the <u>drawing room</u> with Adèle.

3) Jane <u>describes Blanche</u> in detail — she is "<u>accomplished</u>" and "<u>majestic</u>", but has an "arched and <u>haughty</u> lip" and tries to <u>show up</u> one of the other ladies.

4) Mr Rochester seems to <u>ignore</u> Jane, and she is <u>confused</u> and <u>upset</u>. However, he later tells her she must come to the drawing room <u>each evening</u>.

> **Character — Blanche Ingram**
>
> The beautiful Blanche Ingram is dressed in an extravagant "<u>purple riding-habit</u>". She acts as a foil to <u>Jane</u>, as she's got <u>fancy clothes</u>, a shallow mind and wants to marry for <u>money</u> rather than love.

Mr Rochester's guests think they're above Jane

1) The <u>Ingrams</u> talk about "detestable" <u>governesses</u> even though they know Jane is <u>listening</u> — they <u>don't care</u> about <u>hurting</u> her feelings. Lady Ingram criticises Jane's "<u>physiognomy</u>" (facial features) and how it has "the faults of her class", suggesting that Jane is <u>physically inferior</u>.

> **Theme — Social Class**
>
> The Ingrams display <u>snobbery</u> and <u>prejudice</u> towards <u>Jane</u> and the <u>servants</u> at Thornfield. They talk about governesses as if they aren't entitled to the same <u>feelings</u> as other people. The guests believe that they are <u>superior</u> because of their <u>class</u>.

2) <u>Mr Rochester</u> doesn't stop the ladies from <u>criticising</u> governesses, or Jane, and seems to be <u>encouraging</u> Blanche's affection, as they get on well together and she <u>accompanies</u> his singing on the <u>piano</u>.

3) Jane <u>doesn't see</u> the <u>signs</u> that Rochester's <u>interested</u> in <u>her</u>, not Blanche. He asks why she's "depressed" at the end of the evening, and says "Goodnight, my..." as if he was going to call her an <u>affectionate</u> name.

> **KEY QUOTE**
>
> *"...don't mention governesses; the word makes me nervous."*
>
> Blanche, her brother and their mother all speak cruelly about governesses. It sounds like Blanche was a right brat as a child. Personally, I wouldn't be too heartbroken about not being welcomed into their family.

* Most editions of 'Jane Eyre' divide it into 3 volumes. If your edition doesn't, then use the chapter numbers in brackets.

Section Two — Discussion of Chapters

Copyright © BBC Photo Library

Volume Two — Chapters 3-4 (18-19)

These chapters see two unexpected guests at Thornfield — a fortune-teller and a foreigner.

Jane says she isn't jealous of Blanche

1) Jane continues to <u>observe</u> Mr Rochester's guests and keeps a close eye on <u>Blanche</u> and <u>Mr Rochester</u>.

2) She's <u>upset</u> because she's <u>convinced</u> that Mr Rochester is going to <u>marry Blanche</u> and she can't "<u>unlove him</u>".

3) However, Jane thinks Blanche is "too <u>inferior</u> to excite the feeling" of <u>jealousy</u>, and she accepts that Rochester will marry for "<u>family, perhaps political reasons</u>" rather than for <u>love</u>.

© 20TH CENTURY FOX / THE KOBAL COLLECTION

Writer's Techniques

Blanche calls <u>Adèle</u> a "<u>tiresome monkey</u>" and "<u>curled her lip</u>" at Jane. Brontë makes <u>Blanche</u> seem <u>unpleasant</u> to show that if <u>Mr Rochester</u> married her it wouldn't be for <u>love</u>.

Mr Rochester dresses up as a gipsy

1) One evening when <u>Mr Rochester</u> is <u>away</u>, a <u>gipsy</u> turns up at Thornfield and asks to tell the women's <u>fortunes</u>. Each woman sees the gipsy, and finally the gipsy asks for <u>Jane</u>.

2) Jane <u>isn't frightened</u> and answers the gipsy <u>frankly</u> in her normal way. The gipsy tries to find out if she's jealous of Blanche, and mentions the mysterious <u>Grace</u> <u>Poole</u>. She also tells Jane to <u>reach for happiness</u>.

3) The gipsy reveals that she told <u>Blanche</u> that Mr Rochester was <u>not</u> as <u>rich</u> as she thought — Blanche looked "<u>grave</u>" when she heard this, suggesting that she's after a <u>rich husband</u>.

4) The gipsy's <u>voice changes</u>, and it turns out to be Mr Rochester in <u>disguise</u>. Jane is <u>confused</u> by his behaviour, but <u>isn't angry</u> because she feels she <u>hasn't</u> made a <u>fool</u> of herself.

5) The reader realises that Mr Rochester was trying to find out how Jane <u>felt</u> about him, but Jane <u>didn't reveal</u> her <u>true feelings</u>.

Mr Mason's arrival gives Rochester a shock

1) A man called <u>Mr Mason</u> turns up <u>uninvited</u> and asks to see <u>Mr Rochester</u>.

2) Jane thinks that he has an "<u>odd</u> <u>look</u>" and says that his appearance "<u>repelled</u> me <u>exceedingly</u>". He has come from the <u>West Indies</u>.

3) <u>Mr Rochester</u> is <u>disturbed</u> when Jane tells him that Mr Mason has arrived, and he tells her he wishes he was <u>alone</u> on a "<u>quiet island</u>" with her.

4) There is something <u>mysterious</u> about Mr Mason and his relationship with Rochester, but neither the <u>reader nor Jane</u> knows what's going on.

Theme — Foreignness

The fact that <u>Mr Mason</u> lives in <u>Jamaica</u> creates a sense of <u>mystery</u> about him. He breaks the <u>romantic mood</u> between Rochester and Jane here, and it <u>foreshadows</u> the effect of his <u>appearance</u> at Jane and Rochester's <u>wedding</u>.

KEY QUOTE

"the smile on his lips froze"

Mr Rochester has been having some fun by pretending to be a gipsy, but then Mr Mason crashes the party. It's not clear why he's unwelcome, but Mr Rochester goes a bit wobbly and turns white as a sheet. Bizarre.

Section Two — Discussion of Chapters

Volume Two — Chapters 5-7 (20-22)

Mr Rochester got a nasty surprise when Mr Mason arrived, but Mr Mason gets an even nastier surprise...

Mr Mason is attacked in the night

This is a really Gothic scene (see p.59) — the reader doesn't know who or what is in the next room...

1) Everyone is woken up by a loud scream in the night. Mr Rochester convinces his guests that it was a servant's nightmare, but Jane knows it wasn't and Mr Rochester asks her to help the injured Mr Mason.

2) Jane believes that Grace Poole hurt Mr Mason, but agrees to nurse him even though Grace is next door.

3) Mr Mason is treated and sent away. Mr Rochester tells Jane that he made an "error" in a "foreign land". He also asks her to sit with him the night before his marriage and implies he's going to marry Blanche.

Theme — Secrecy and Deception

Rochester won't let Jane and Mr Mason talk to each other. Mr Mason clearly knows something that Mr Rochester doesn't want Jane (or his other guests) to know about.

Jane is summoned to Gateshead

1) Bessie's husband arrives to tell Jane that her cousin John is dead and that her aunt keeps asking for her. Rochester reluctantly allows her to go, as long as she promises to return.

2) When Jane arrives at Gateshead, she isn't intimidated by Eliza and Georgiana. She insists on going to see her aunt, who is dying.

3) Jane is kind to Aunt Reed — she apologises for her behaviour as a child and offers her aunt her "full and free forgiveness", but Mrs Reed remains bitter towards Jane.

4) Jane discovers that her uncle in Madeira wrote to Mrs Reed three years ago wishing to adopt Jane, but she told him Jane was dead, because she didn't want Jane to have a happy life.

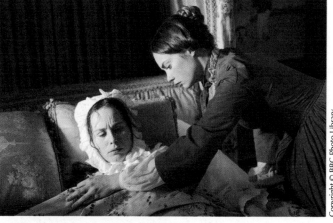

Copyright © BBC Photo Library

Character — Jane

Jane's kindness to Mrs Reed shows how much she has matured since leaving Gateshead. She is able to forgive her unhappy childhood and wants to be reconciled with her family.

Mrs Reed dies and Jane goes 'home'

1) Mrs Reed dies, and Jane returns to Thornfield a month later. She feels as if she's returning "home" for the first time in her life, and has to keep reminding herself that it's not really her home.

2) She believes that Mr Rochester will get married soon, but they spend a lot of time together and both seem happy.

Writer's Techniques — Language

The narration switches into the present tense when Jane arrives at Thornfield: "I see — Mr Rochester". It gives the reader the impression that Jane vividly remembers being reunited with Mr Rochester, and the reader feels as if they are there with her.

Write about how Jane's behaviour changes during the novel...

Jane's grown up, so she apologises to her aunt for her actions. Mrs Reed, however, never grows out of being bitter and resentful. She only confesses about the letter because she's scared of going to hell if she doesn't.

Volume Two — Chapters 8-9 (23-24)

Hands up who saw this one coming — Mr Rochester proposes to Jane, not Blanche Ingram.

Mr Rochester asks Jane to marry him

1) Jane goes for a walk in the garden and is followed by Mr Rochester.

2) Rochester teases her by saying he's going to marry Blanche and Jane will have to leave. Jane tells him passionately that she doesn't want to leave him.

3) When he stops teasing her, Rochester tells Jane that he wants to marry her. Jane doesn't believe him, but after a while he convinces her to accept.

© ITV/REX

Theme — Gender

Jane sees herself as Rochester's equal and accepts his proposal on those terms, which was unusual for women in the 19th century. Jane tells him that she is "no bird" and she wants to be free to decide her own destiny.

The weather foreshadows an unhappy event

1) Just after Jane accepts Mr Rochester's proposal, the weather changes and it starts to rain. The horse-chestnut tree "writhed and groaned" and the "wind roared".

2) The next day they discover that the horse-chestnut tree where they'd sitting has been split in half by lightning.

Writer's Techniques

This is an example of pathetic fallacy (see p.60) — where an author gives human emotions to nature or objects. The pathetic fallacy here foreshadows something dreadful — the stormy weather suggests that their wedding won't go smoothly.

Mrs Fairfax doesn't approve of the marriage

Background and Context

Mrs Fairfax is the voice of social expectations here — she believes that Mr Rochester should marry someone of "equal position and fortune".

1) Mrs Fairfax tells Jane she disapproves of the engagement.

2) She tells Jane to keep him "at a distance". She says that "Gentlemen in his station are not accustomed to marrying their governesses."

Character — Mr Rochester

Mr Rochester is happy to ignore social conventions and marry Jane rather than Blanche. However, trying to buy Jane expensive presents suggests that he doesn't understand Jane — he makes her uncomfortable and emphasises the difference in their fortunes.

3) Jane asks Mr Rochester why he pretended he was going to marry Blanche, and he says it was to make Jane jealous. Jane is concerned about Blanche's feelings, but Mr Rochester is sure that Blanche thought that he wasn't rich enough for her.

4) Mr Rochester wants to give Jane jewels and buy her fancy dresses — it all makes her feel very uncomfortable.

5) Jane says that she's lost sight of God and "made an idol" of Rochester — this is another hint that this marriage might not be the best idea.

"I am no bird; and no net ensnares me"

Jane makes sure that Mr Rochester knows she isn't going to be a conventional wife — she wants to be his equal. However, lightning and Mrs Fairfax both suggest that trouble may be ahead... watch out, Jane!

Volume Two — Chapters 10-11 (25-26)

Everyone loves a good wedding — there's the dress, the cake, the brother of your secret wife...

Everything is ready for the wedding

1) Jane has <u>packed</u> her <u>belongings</u>, ready to <u>leave</u> after the <u>wedding</u>.

2) She is <u>restless</u>, and goes into the <u>garden</u>. She goes to the <u>horse-chestnut tree</u> where Mr Rochester <u>proposed</u> to her, and sees that the "<u>halves</u> were <u>not broken</u> from each other".

Writer's Techniques

Brontë uses the tree as a <u>symbol</u> for Rochester and Jane's <u>relationship</u>. Just as the tree was hit by <u>lightning</u>, the relationship is about to be <u>seemingly destroyed</u>. But the <u>two halves</u> of the tree are <u>clinging</u> on to each other, so there may be a <u>future</u> for Jane and Rochester.

3) Mr Rochester has been <u>away</u>, and when he returns Jane tells him she had <u>bad dreams</u> and saw a "<u>savage</u>" in her room when she woke in the <u>night</u>, who ripped her <u>wedding veil</u>. Mr Rochester initially says it <u>wasn't real</u>, but then blames it on <u>Grace Poole</u> — the reader can see he's <u>deceiving</u> her, but Jane seems <u>blinded</u> by love.

4) Mr Rochester tells Jane to spend the night with <u>Adèle</u> so that she won't be <u>scared</u>. However, he's actually <u>worried</u> that Jane might be in <u>danger</u> in her <u>own room</u>.

The wedding is interrupted

KEY EVENT

1) Mr Rochester <u>hurries</u> Jane to the <u>church</u> in a "grasp of iron" and says they'll leave <u>straight</u> afterwards.

2) Jane sees two <u>unknown figures</u> in the churchyard, but Mr Rochester <u>doesn't notice</u> them.

3) Rochester's <u>urgency</u> and the <u>appearance</u> of these <u>people</u> gives the reader a pretty <u>bad feeling</u> about the <u>wedding</u>.

4) The wedding is <u>interrupted</u> by a <u>solicitor</u>, who says that Mr Rochester already has a <u>wife</u>, called <u>Bertha</u>. This is confirmed by the man with him, who turns out to be <u>Mr Mason</u> — <u>Bertha's brother</u>.

5) This is the <u>mystery</u> that Mr Rochester has been <u>hiding</u> — Bertha has been living at Thornfield all along.

© AF archive/Alamy

Jane meets Bertha

1) Rochester takes <u>Jane</u>, the <u>two men</u> and the <u>priest</u> to the <u>attic</u>, where they see the <u>wild Bertha</u>. Bertha attacks Mr Rochester "<u>viciously</u>", but he <u>doesn't fight back</u>, just <u>restrains</u> her, and she is soon "bound" to a chair.

Character — Bertha Mason

Bertha is described as a terrifying <u>beast</u>. She has a "<u>fierce</u> cry" and is called a "clothed <u>hyena</u>", "<u>maniac</u>" and "<u>lunatic</u>", as well as having "<u>shaggy locks</u>" and a "<u>purple</u> face". Brontë <u>piles up</u> these <u>descriptions</u> to create a <u>grotesque</u> picture of Bertha.

2) Jane had <u>written</u> to her <u>uncle</u> in Madeira to tell him about the <u>wedding</u>, and by chance, he was with <u>Mr Mason</u> at the time. Mr Mason knew that Mr Rochester was already <u>married</u>, so travelled back to England to <u>stop</u> the wedding.

3) Jane describes herself as a "<u>cold, solitary girl again</u>" — she's lost everything.

KEY QUOTE

"...the clothed hyena rose up, and stood tall on its hind-feet."

The mystery is revealed and the wedding is ruined — it turns out Mr Rochester's been hiding his mad wife, Bertha, on the third floor. Bertha's often described as an animal or supernatural creature. Creepy stuff.

Volume Three — Chapter 1 (27)

Jane has a pretty difficult decision to make — should she stay, or should she go?

Jane wrestles with her feelings

Volume Two ends with a bit of a bombshell — the tension is released, but the reader wonders what Jane will do now.

1) Jane has <u>hidden</u> herself away in her room and desperately tries to <u>decide</u> what to do. Part of her tells her to <u>leave</u> Thornfield straight away, but part of her says she <u>can't</u>.

2) She realises that she must <u>help herself</u> and make her own decision about what to do next. Even though she <u>knows</u> she will <u>suffer</u>, she finally decides she <u>has</u> to <u>leave</u>.

3) As she leaves her room she almost <u>faints</u>, but is <u>caught</u> by Mr Rochester who's been <u>waiting</u> for her.

Mr Rochester tries to explain his side of the story

1) Mr Rochester invites Jane to get <u>angry</u> or <u>upset</u> with him. He <u>apologises</u> to her with "deep remorse" and although she doesn't tell him, Jane <u>forgives</u> him at her "heart's core".

2) Rochester <u>doesn't accept</u> that Jane <u>wants</u> to <u>leave</u> him, and he tries to <u>persuade</u> her to <u>live</u> with him even though they <u>aren't married</u>.

3) He suggests that he was <u>misled</u> into marrying Bertha by his father and brother. The marriage was unhappy, due to Bertha's many "vices", and then she was declared <u>insane</u>. Although he has tried to do the <u>right thing</u> for Bertha, he has always been looking for <u>real love</u>.

> **Writer's Techniques**
>
> Brontë allows Mr Rochester to take over the <u>narrative</u>, giving the reader an <u>insight</u> into his <u>younger</u> character. This also helps the reader to feel more <u>sympathetic</u> towards him.

4) He mentions that he had <u>several mistresses</u>, but saw them as "<u>inferior</u>" and "hates the recollection" of the time he spent with them. Jane believes that he would eventually think the <u>same</u> about her if she agreed to be his mistress.

5) He describes the <u>impact</u> that Jane had on him from the moment he <u>first</u> met her. He <u>loves</u> Jane and asks her to stay with him and be <u>faithful</u> to him.

For more about morality, see p.46.

> **Theme — Rochester's Morality**
>
> Rochester believes that Jane should <u>live</u> with him, even though they <u>can't</u> get <u>married</u>. He seems to <u>ignore</u>, or <u>not care</u> about, the <u>moral implications</u> of Jane being his <u>mistress</u>.

> **Theme — Jane's Morality**
>
> Although she deeply <u>loves</u> Rochester and forgives him, Jane <u>won't</u> live as his <u>mistress</u>. Her <u>moral values</u> mean that she believes this would be <u>wrong</u>.

Jane leaves Thornfield

1) Mr Rochester is <u>heartbroken</u> when he realises that Jane is going to leave him. Jane is also <u>heartbroken</u> and is <u>afraid</u> that Mr Rochester will go back to a <u>life of sin</u>. She creeps out of Thornfield, taking very little with her.

2) She wants to <u>turn back</u> to Thornfield, but <u>doesn't</u>, and takes a <u>coach</u> as <u>far away</u> as possible.

© AF archive/Alamy

Write about how Jane does what she believes is right...

Jane would save herself some heartbreak (and hunger) if she stayed at Thornfield. But she wouldn't respect herself if she did — for her, getting married is the only way they can be together. So off she goes...

Volume Three — Chapters 2-4 (28-30)

Jane has left Mr Rochester and Thornfield behind — so we're going to need some new characters...

Jane comes close to death

© iStockphoto.com/Danielrao

1) Jane spends all her <u>money</u> on the coach journey, and then accidentally <u>leaves</u> her <u>belongings</u> behind.

2) She spends time <u>wandering</u> around the <u>moors</u> and <u>sleeps</u> there for two nights, <u>hungry</u> and <u>sad</u>.

3) She <u>can't find</u> any <u>work</u>, and is forced to <u>beg</u> for some bread. In desperate need of <u>shelter</u>, she heads towards the <u>lights</u> of a <u>house</u> she can see in the <u>dark</u>. At the house, she watches <u>three women</u> through the window, but is <u>turned away</u> by the <u>housekeeper</u>.

4) Jane sits on the <u>doorstep</u> and <u>thinks</u> she is going to <u>die</u>, until she's <u>rescued</u> and taken inside by <u>St. John Rivers</u>.

Writer's Techniques

The moors are a <u>wild</u>, <u>rugged</u> and <u>beautiful</u> area of <u>countryside</u>. They represent Jane's new <u>freedom</u>, but also the <u>lack of security</u> she now has.

Jane is welcomed into the Rivers family

1) Jane's <u>ill</u> in bed for a few days and the <u>Rivers family</u> look after her. They wonder <u>who</u> she is and <u>what's happened</u>. Once she's <u>better</u> she tells them some of her <u>story</u>, but <u>not</u> her <u>real name</u>.

2) The two sisters, <u>Diana</u> and <u>Mary</u>, are very <u>kind</u> to Jane. Their brother, <u>St. John</u>, is <u>less sympathetic</u>, but says he will <u>help</u> her to find work.

3) Even though Jane is <u>reliant</u> on the family and <u>grateful</u> for their help, she talks to them as <u>equals</u> and <u>doesn't</u> tell them more than she <u>wants</u> to.

Character — St. John

St. John is a <u>clergyman</u> and often comes across as a <u>serious</u> and <u>impersonal</u> character. However, he <u>saves</u> Jane's <u>life</u> and has the <u>kindness</u> to let her stay in his house.

Diana and Mary enjoy having Jane around

1) Jane, Diana and Mary <u>get on</u> very well together, and life at <u>Moor House</u> is a new <u>experience</u> for Jane. She has <u>real friends</u> for the first time since she was at Lowood, and she <u>feels</u> at <u>home</u>.

2) Their brother, <u>St. John</u>, <u>intrigues</u> Jane — she thinks that he <u>isn't happy</u> and is <u>looking</u> for <u>something</u> that he <u>hasn't found</u> yet. He believes that God has <u>called</u> him to be a <u>missionary</u>, and is waiting to go <u>overseas</u>.

3) St. John asks Jane if she will become a local <u>schoolteacher</u>. He is <u>worried</u> that she will find the job <u>beneath</u> her, but she <u>gladly accepts</u> it.

4) The Rivers family receive a <u>letter</u> which tells them that their <u>uncle</u> has <u>died</u>. St. John reports that the uncle has left his fortune to "the <u>other relation</u>", who isn't named...

Mention that Jane clearly belongs with the Rivers sisters...

Even before she's met them, Jane admires the sisters' bookish ways, and once they get to know each other, they're like three peas in a pod. Then there's that letter hinting at a long-lost relative — who could that be?

Volume Three — Chapters 5-7 (31-33)

Jane is back on her feet and ready to start a new life as a teacher in the small village of Morton.

Jane has a new home

Life seems to have settled down for Jane, but the reader is very aware that she still loves Mr Rochester.

1) Jane moves into a small <u>cottage</u> in <u>Morton</u> and starts a new life <u>teaching</u> the girls in the village. However, she finds it <u>hard</u> and is <u>shocked</u> by the "<u>poverty</u>" and "<u>ignorance</u>" of the <u>children</u>.

2) She <u>feels</u> that she's <u>gone down</u> in the <u>world</u>, and <u>questions</u> whether she made the right <u>decision</u> not to stay with <u>Mr Rochester</u>. However, she does think that on a <u>moral level</u> she made the "<u>correct choice</u>".

3) <u>St. John</u> realises Jane is <u>sad</u> and tells her not to "<u>look back</u>" He explains that he was <u>unhappy</u> before he decided to follow what he thinks is <u>God's will</u> for his life, by becoming a <u>missionary</u>.

4) <u>Miss Oliver</u> visits Jane. She's the <u>beautiful</u> daughter of a <u>rich</u> local man. She seems to <u>like</u> St. John, but he tries to <u>avoid</u> contact with her and is <u>reluctant</u> to <u>spend time</u> with her.

Jane works hard at the school

1) Jane <u>works calmly</u> at the village <u>school</u> and starts to <u>enjoy</u> her <u>new life</u>. But she spends her <u>nights dreaming</u> of <u>Mr Rochester</u>.

2) <u>Miss Oliver</u> often visits the school and becomes <u>friendly</u> with Jane.

3) Jane asks <u>St. John</u> about his <u>feelings</u> for Miss Oliver. He seems to <u>love</u> her, but he can't imagine <u>her</u> as a <u>missionary's wife</u>, and <u>he</u> won't <u>give up</u> his "<u>great work</u>" to stay with her. He's putting his <u>ambition</u> to do <u>God's work</u> above his <u>personal happiness</u>.

St. John discovers who Jane is

KEY EVENT

1) The next day, <u>St. John</u> tells Jane a <u>story</u> about a <u>poor curate</u> and the <u>daughter</u> of a <u>rich man</u>, who got <u>married</u>, had a <u>daughter</u> and <u>died</u>. As he continues, Jane quickly <u>realises</u> that the story is about <u>her</u>.

Theme — Family

Jane finds out that she has <u>inherited</u> a <u>huge</u> amount of <u>money</u>, and "independence would be glorious", but the discovery that she is <u>related</u> to the Rivers is far more <u>important</u> to her. She calls this discovery "<u>wealth</u> to the <u>heart</u>" and "<u>exhilarating</u>".

2) Jane <u>hopes</u> that this means St. John has discovered some <u>news</u> about <u>Mr Rochester</u> for her, but he <u>hasn't</u> and she is <u>disappointed</u>.

3) St John has worked out that Jane is the <u>relative</u> mentioned in the <u>letter</u> that the Rivers family received. He tells Jane that she has <u>inherited £20 000</u> — she is very <u>rich</u>.

4) This means that the Rivers siblings are her <u>cousins</u> (bit of a coincidence). Jane is <u>very happy</u> to suddenly have a <u>family</u>, and decides to <u>share</u> her <u>inheritance</u> equally between all <u>four</u> of them, as a "legacy of life, hope, enjoyment".

KEY QUOTE

"This was a blessing..."

She's been hiding her identity from the Rivers family, but St. John finds out more about Jane than she knew herself. When Jane gains cousins and a fortune, it's the sense of belonging that really makes her happy.

Volume Three — Chapters 8-10 (34-36)

St. John Rivers has a starring role in these chapters — he asks Jane to marry him and go to India with him.

Jane refuses to marry St. John

This is a key moment — St. John's proposal forces Jane to make a decision about her future.

1) Jane is still "craving" to hear about <u>Mr Rochester</u>. She writes <u>two letters</u> to Mrs Fairfax asking about <u>him</u>, but gets <u>no reply</u> — she's very <u>disappointed</u>.

2) <u>St. John</u> asks Jane to learn <u>Hindustani</u> (an Indian/Pakistani language) and later asks her to <u>marry</u> him and go to <u>India</u> to <u>help</u> him as a <u>missionary</u>. Part of Jane thinks she should go, but they <u>don't love</u> each other, and she <u>doesn't want</u> a <u>loveless marriage</u>. It's almost the opposite of the situation when she left Mr Rochester.

Theme — Marriage

Jane tries to bend <u>social conventions</u> here. She wants to travel with St. John <u>pretending</u> to be his <u>sister</u>, but he is <u>adamant</u> that it would only be <u>right</u> if she was his <u>wife</u>.

3) Jane tells St. John that she <u>will go</u> with him, but <u>not</u> as his <u>wife</u>. St. John <u>refuses</u> — he <u>feels</u> it'd be <u>improper</u> and he wants a wife he can "influence" and "retain".

Theme — Freedom

Jane says that she will go to <u>India</u> if she "may go <u>free</u>". Jane has found <u>financial freedom</u> thanks to her uncle's inheritance, and she <u>doesn't want</u> to give up her <u>personal freedom</u> by <u>marrying</u> a man she <u>doesn't love</u>.

St. John believes he knows better than Jane

1) Jane <u>stands up</u> for herself <u>against</u> St. John, who is <u>shocked</u> by her words and her thoughts. He <u>describes</u> her words as "<u>inexcusable</u>" and "<u>unfeminine</u>", but Jane sees herself as his <u>equal</u>.

2) When Jane talks to Diana about the proposal, Diana agrees that <u>marrying</u> him <u>without love</u> would be "<u>out of the question</u>".

3) Jane begins to <u>change</u> her mind, and asks God to show her "the path". At the <u>last minute</u>, she hears a <u>mysterious voice calling</u> her name. It sounds like <u>Mr Rochester</u>, and she decides to go to Thornfield to find him.

Theme — The Supernatural

Just like the "<u>fairy</u>" that suggested <u>advertising</u> as a <u>governess</u>, it is a <u>supernatural</u> incident that <u>leads</u> Jane back to <u>Mr Rochester</u>.

Jane has to find out what's happened to Mr Rochester

1) <u>Jane</u> sets off for <u>Thornfield</u>, but when she gets there the <u>house</u> has been <u>burnt down</u> and she <u>worries</u> that <u>Rochester</u> might be <u>dead</u>.

2) She goes to the <u>local inn</u> and hears that Rochester is still <u>alive</u>. <u>Bertha</u> set <u>fire</u> to the house, but Mr Rochester <u>saved</u> the servants. He <u>tried</u> to save <u>Bertha</u> too, but she <u>jumped off</u> the <u>roof</u>.

3) The fire blinded Mr Rochester and he <u>lost</u> his <u>left hand</u>. He left Thornfield, sent <u>Adèle</u> to <u>boarding school</u> and now lives <u>thirty miles</u> away at <u>Ferndean</u>. Jane sets off to see him <u>straight away</u>.

Comment on the importance of the minor characters...

We usually just hear Jane's side of the story, but as Jane wasn't there, the innkeeper tells Jane (and us) about the fire and Mr Rochester's injuries. He's pretty important to fill in all the gaps in the story here...

Volume Three — Chapters 11-12 (37-38)

Jane makes the last of her long journeys in the novel — this time to find the man she loves.

Jane and Mr Rochester are reunited at Ferndean

1) Jane walks through the <u>cold</u>, <u>wet</u> and <u>gloomy woods</u> to <u>Ferndean</u>. She thinks she's <u>lost</u>, but finally finds the "<u>desolate</u> spot" where the <u>house</u> is.

2) She <u>watches</u> Mr Rochester come out of the <u>front door</u> but stays hidden. After he has gone in, she's <u>let in</u> by the housekeeper.

3) Jane <u>takes</u> Mr Rochester a drink and he <u>can't believe</u> it's her. Because he is <u>blind</u>, at first he thinks she's a "delusion" — not <u>real</u>.

4) She <u>isn't</u> put off by his <u>damaged</u> hand or the fact that he is <u>blind</u>, even though he <u>thinks</u> she will be. Instead, she says that she will <u>always look after him</u>.

They get to know each other again...

Mr Rochester tells Jane he called out for her and heard her reply — at exactly the time Jane thought she heard him. See p.51 for more on the supernatural elements in the novel.

1) Mr Rochester gets up <u>early</u> the next day because he <u>can't wait</u> to meet <u>Jane</u> again.

2) They spend the day <u>together</u> and Mr Rochester wants to <u>know</u> all about <u>Jane's time away</u> from him.

3) Jane tells him about her <u>cousins</u>, and Mr Rochester is <u>jealous</u> of St. John, believing that Jane <u>wanted</u> to <u>marry</u> him. Jane <u>teases</u> him, but makes him <u>realise</u> that she wants to <u>marry</u> him, and he <u>proposes</u> to her <u>again</u>.

Character — Jane

Jane <u>teases</u> Rochester about <u>St. John</u>, just as he <u>teased</u> her about marrying <u>Blanche</u>. This shows that the <u>equality</u> Jane wanted in their <u>relationship</u> has been <u>achieved</u>. Jane is also now <u>financially independent</u>, so she <u>doesn't</u> have to <u>rely</u> on Rochester's <u>money</u>.

...and live happily ever after

The novel ends ten years after Jane and Rochester get married — this gap is when Jane is writing her story.

1) Jane and Mr Rochester have a <u>quiet wedding</u> and feel "supremely blest" with their marriage.

2) They have a <u>son</u> and Mr Rochester <u>regains sight</u> in <u>one eye</u>. <u>Adèle</u> has been looked after, and is a good companion to Jane.

3) Brontë treats Mr Rochester in a biblical way at the end — he's physically punished for his sins, but he's <u>rewarded</u> for trying to <u>save Bertha</u>, seeking a <u>quieter life</u> and being a <u>faithful husband</u> to <u>Jane</u>.

Theme — Marriage

<u>Jane</u>, <u>Diana</u> and <u>Mary</u> are all <u>rewarded</u> for believing that they should <u>marry</u> for <u>love</u>. Brontë <u>finishes</u> the novel with all <u>three</u> of them <u>happily married</u>.

4) <u>Diana</u> and <u>Mary</u> have also got <u>married</u> and keep in touch with <u>Jane</u>.

5) The book <u>ends</u> with Jane talking about <u>St. John</u> and his <u>work</u> in <u>India</u>. He is <u>dying</u>, but she is glad that he is <u>fulfilling</u> God's will. <u>St. John's words</u> conclude the <u>final paragraph</u> — he is <u>ready</u> to be with <u>God</u>, and Brontë seems to <u>commend</u> him for <u>sacrificing</u> his <u>life</u> for <u>God</u>.

KEY QUOTE

"Reader, I married him."

The final chapter opens with this famous quote — after a complicated love story, Jane finally makes herself Mrs Rochester. About time too — it's been a stressful few hundred pages — my nails are bitten to shreds.

Section Two — Discussion of Chapters

Practice Questions

There you have it — 'Jane Eyre' in a nutshell. It's a pretty long book with a lot going on, so have a go at these questions to see how much you've taken in. You only need to write about a line for each question — simple.

Quick Questions

1) Who does Jane live with at the start of the novel?

2) How is Jane punished for fighting with John Reed?

3) What aspect of Jane's journey to Lowood surprises the staff on her arrival?

4) What does Helen Burns die of?

5) What event prompts Jane to decide to leave Lowood and become a governess?

6) How does Mrs Fairfax describe Mr Rochester?

7) Why does Mr Rochester need Jane's help when they first meet?

8) What is Blanche Ingram's attitude towards governesses?

9) Why do you think Mr Rochester dresses up as a gipsy?

10) Why does Jane return to Gateshead?

Practice Questions

Quick Questions

11) How does Mrs Fairfax feel about Jane's engagement to Mr Rochester?

12) Who interrupts the wedding, and why?

13) What does Mr Rochester think he and Jane should do if they can't get married?

14) Who helps Jane when she's starving and has nowhere to go?

15) Why does St. John think that Jane might refuse his offer of employment?

16) Why does Jane find working at Morton School difficult?

17) What two pieces of good news come from St. John discovering Jane's true identity?

18) Why does Jane refuse to marry St. John?

19) What injuries did Mr Rochester get during the fire at Thornfield?

20) What happens to Diana, Mary and St. John Rivers at the end of the novel?

Practice Questions

The last stop before you can dive into a section of character analysis is this page of In-depth Questions. You should be aiming to write about a paragraph for each answer — well, go on then, get cracking.

In-depth Questions

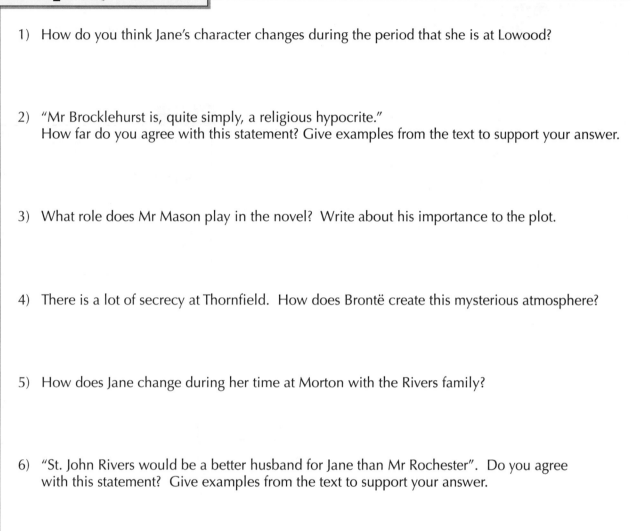

1) How do you think Jane's character changes during the period that she is at Lowood?

2) "Mr Brocklehurst is, quite simply, a religious hypocrite."
   How far do you agree with this statement? Give examples from the text to support your answer.

3) What role does Mr Mason play in the novel? Write about his importance to the plot.

4) There is a lot of secrecy at Thornfield. How does Brontë create this mysterious atmosphere?

5) How does Jane change during her time at Morton with the Rivers family?

6) "St. John Rivers would be a better husband for Jane than Mr Rochester". Do you agree with this statement? Give examples from the text to support your answer.

7) Mr Rochester lies, takes mistresses and tries to marry Jane when he's already married.
   Does he deserve to marry Jane and be happy at the end of the novel?
   Support your answer with examples from the text.

Character Profile — Jane Eyre

The first character page is all about Jane — bet you didn't see that one coming...

Jane is the narrator and the protagonist

© Moviestore collection Ltd/Alamy

1) Jane is the <u>protagonist</u> (main character) in the novel and the <u>story</u> is <u>narrated</u> by her. The novel <u>focuses</u> on her <u>relationships</u> with other characters and the way her character <u>progresses</u>.

2) *Jane Eyre* is a <u>bildungsroman</u> (see p.59). This means the novel explores Jane's <u>personal</u> and <u>moral development</u> as she <u>grows up</u>.

3) Jane is <u>passionate</u> and <u>strong-willed</u>, which was <u>unusual</u> at the time -— women were expected to be <u>modest</u> and not hold or express <u>strong feelings</u> or <u>emotions</u>.

4) She's also <u>hard-working</u> and keen to <u>improve</u> herself through <u>learning</u> — St. John admires her <u>work ethic</u> and "unflagging energy".

Jane is...

An outsider: "there she is still, behind the window-curtain."

Independent: "I am no bird; and no net ensnares me; I am a free human being with an independent will"

Strong-willed: "I don't think, sir, you have a right to command me, merely because you are older than I".

She is often an outsider...

1) Jane <u>begins</u> the novel as an <u>orphan</u> living with her <u>aunt</u> and <u>cousins</u>, who <u>don't like</u> or <u>love</u> her.

2) They think that she is "<u>naughty</u>" and "<u>passionate</u>", and even the <u>servants</u> have a "<u>bad opinion</u>" of her. In fact, she <u>tries</u> to be <u>good</u> and keep out of <u>trouble</u>, but she's <u>tormented</u> by her cousins — particularly <u>John</u>.

3) <u>Mr Brocklehurst</u> tries to make Jane an outsider at <u>Lowood</u> by <u>claiming</u> that she is a "<u>liar</u>".

4) At <u>Thornfield</u>, Jane is caught <u>between</u> the <u>servants</u> and the <u>upper-class guests</u> — she doesn't <u>fit in</u> with either group, making her an outsider.

Writer's Techniques

Jane's status as an <u>outsider</u> at Thornfield means that she spends lots of time <u>observing</u> other people, which aids her <u>narrative</u> — she sees <u>all</u> that goes on between the guests, and <u>shares</u> this with the reader.

5) When she <u>leaves</u> Thornfield, Jane is <u>alone</u>, has <u>no social status</u>, <u>begs</u> for food and <u>nearly dies</u> — she is completely <u>outside</u> of society before the Rivers family take her in.

...but ends up with a family

For more on Jane's desire for a family, see p.44.

1) Jane has a strong desire to <u>belong</u> and becomes <u>less</u> of an <u>outsider</u> as the novel <u>progresses</u>.

2) Things begin to <u>change</u> at <u>Lowood</u> — Jane makes <u>friends</u> with <u>Helen Burns</u>, and <u>Miss Temple</u> looks after her.

3) Jane <u>battles</u> through the <u>hardships</u> at Lowood — enduring the poor conditions and eventually becoming a <u>teacher</u> there. This <u>enables</u> her to <u>move on</u> and become a <u>governess</u>.

4) At <u>Thornfield</u>, she has a <u>family of sorts</u> — she likes <u>Mr Rochester</u>, <u>Mrs Fairfax</u> and <u>Adèle</u>, but must <u>leave</u> them.

Theme — Family

<u>Mary</u> and <u>Diana</u> have <u>similar interests</u> to Jane, and are <u>closer</u> to her than any <u>other women</u> in the novel — it seems right that they turn out to be <u>related</u> to her.

5) Jane's filled with "sudden <u>joy</u>" when she finds out she's related to the Rivers family. Having <u>relations</u> is far more <u>important</u> to her than the <u>money</u> she also finds out about.

6) At the end, Jane <u>marries</u> Rochester, they begin their <u>own family</u> and Jane finally has somewhere she <u>belongs</u> completely.

kehyeeaa

Character Profile — Jane Eyre

Jane has to balance conflicting characteristics and desires

Passion -vs- Self-control

- Jane is <u>passionate</u> — she deeply loves Mr Rochester and <u>fights</u> against sadness and jealousy when it looks like he'll marry Blanche Ingram. She also <u>shocks</u> St. John with her passionate, "<u>unfeminine</u>" words".
- However, she tries to be <u>self-controlled</u> — she manages to <u>hide</u> her feelings when questioned by the <u>fortune-teller</u>.

Independence -vs- Desire to belong

- Jane can be <u>independent</u> and she isn't afraid to <u>stand up</u> for herself — she <u>rebels</u> against the Reeds and she makes <u>tough decisions</u> to leave Mr Rochester and St. John, even though they both try to <u>persuade</u> her against it.
- However, this independence <u>clashes</u> with her desire to <u>belong</u> — she ultimately <u>returns</u> to Mr Rochester.

She has strong ideas about right and wrong

1) When Jane <u>finds out</u> that Mr Rochester is already <u>married</u>, she knows she can't become his <u>mistress</u>. Even though she is <u>desperate</u> to be with him, she <u>won't</u> go against what she <u>believes</u> to be <u>right</u>.

2) She's also <u>caring</u> — she <u>tells off</u> Mr Rochester for speaking <u>unkindly</u> about Bertha — "she cannot help being mad", and is <u>concerned</u> for Blanche's <u>feelings</u> after Mr Rochester <u>rejects</u> her.

3) As <u>Mrs Reed</u> is <u>dying</u>, Jane <u>apologises</u> to her and offers her "full and free <u>forgiveness</u>" — she's keen to put <u>right</u> past <u>wrongs</u> and not dwell on <u>bitterness</u>.

Theme — Morality

<u>Helen Burns</u> (see p.38) helps Jane to realise that <u>forgiveness</u> is <u>better</u> than <u>bitterness</u>, allowing Jane to <u>forgive</u> Mrs Reed.

4) Jane is <u>religious</u> (see p.45) and has <u>strong Christian morals</u>. She seems prepared to <u>sacrifice</u> her life and happiness for <u>God</u> and go to India, but ultimately her <u>passion</u> leads her back to Mr Rochester.

Jane and Rochester have an unconventional relationship

1) Mr Rochester talks about Jane as if she's a <u>fairy-tale creature</u>. He calls her a "malicious <u>elf</u>" and jokingly <u>accuses</u> her of putting a <u>curse</u> on his <u>horse</u>.

2) He also <u>teases</u> Jane so much that she tells him that she's not "a <u>machine</u> without <u>feelings</u>".

3) Jane's <u>ambiguous social position</u> also complicates things — she's not a <u>servant</u>, but she is <u>employed</u> by <u>Mr Rochester</u> and isn't <u>socially equal</u> to him.

4) <u>Neither</u> Jane nor Mr Rochester are <u>physically attractive</u>. Jane describes herself as being "<u>plain</u>, and <u>little</u>", and she tells Mr Rochester that he <u>isn't handsome</u>. This is <u>unusual</u> for the main <u>romantic couple</u> in a 19th-century novel.

© ITV/REX

KEY QUOTE

"He had not imagined that a woman would dare to speak so"

Jane shocks a few people with her passion and strong feelings — Mr Rochester loves it, but St. John doesn't really know how to deal with her. Probably a good thing she ends up marrying Mr Rochester really...

Character Profile — Mr Rochester

Mr Rochester isn't your average rich gentleman — he's a man of secrets and mystery...

Mr Rochester is an intriguing character

1) Edward Fairfax Rochester is the eccentric <u>master</u> of <u>Thornfield</u>. He brings <u>excitement</u> to Jane's life, but also <u>breaks</u> her <u>heart</u>.

2) Mr Rochester and Jane fall in <u>love</u>, but he's a lot <u>older</u> than she is, and she's both his <u>employee</u> and <u>beneath him</u> in terms of <u>class</u>.

3) He had <u>relationships</u> in <u>Europe</u> but never found his "<u>ideal</u> of a <u>woman</u>". <u>19th-century gentlemen</u> often had <u>mistresses</u>, but Rochester <u>confesses</u> that his lifestyle was <u>sinful</u>.

4) He's the <u>guardian</u> of <u>Adèle Varens</u> — the <u>daughter</u> of a <u>French</u> dancer who Mr Rochester had an <u>affair</u> with.

> **Mr Rochester is...**
>
> **Troubled**: "an agony of inward contempt masters me."
>
> **Secretive**: "Mr Rochester stepped out of his disguise."
>
> **Masterful**: "The new face was... dark, strong, and stern."

> **Theme — Family**
>
> Mr Rochester's <u>unhappiness</u> also seems to have been caused by <u>family</u> members, creating a <u>parallel</u> with Jane.

5) It also turns out that he's <u>married</u> to a woman called <u>Bertha Mason</u>, who he met in <u>Jamaica</u>. His <u>family arranged</u> their marriage for <u>money</u>, and he's <u>regretted</u> it ever since because she is <u>insane</u>.

6) He seems to <u>change</u> after Jane leaves him — he <u>honourably</u> and <u>bravely</u> tries to save Bertha, and he is <u>repentant</u> of his past behaviour.

© Moviestore/REX

In some ways, he's a conventional gentleman...

1) Mr Rochester is a <u>wealthy</u>, upper-class gentleman — he's the master of <u>Thornfield</u> and the <u>land</u> around it, and he owns <u>Ferndean</u>, another house.

2) He has lived in <u>exotic</u> locations, e.g. <u>Jamaica</u>, and enjoyed the <u>lifestyle</u> of a <u>wealthy gentleman</u> in Europe — including having mistresses.

3) He spends time with <u>aristocratic friends</u>, who come to stay at Thornfield. He's at <u>ease</u> in their company and seems to enjoy <u>entertaining</u> them.

4) He <u>appears</u> keen to follow social expectations and <u>marry</u> an <u>aristocratic beauty</u> (Blanche Ingram), although he's actually only interested in Jane.

5) He likes to display his <u>wealth</u> — after <u>Jane</u> accepts his marriage <u>proposal</u>, he wants to dress her up like a "<u>doll</u>" with <u>fine dresses</u> and <u>expensive jewels</u>.

...but he's also unconventional

1) Mr Rochester is <u>unpredictable</u>, and it's often <u>difficult</u> to work out if he is being <u>serious</u> or <u>not</u>. He can be <u>cynical</u> and <u>controlling</u>, and Jane thinks he's "<u>strikingly peculiar</u>" after she first spends time with him.

2) It's obvious to the <u>reader</u> that he's hiding a <u>dark secret</u> — this makes it <u>difficult</u> to <u>trust</u> him.

3) He <u>confides</u> in Jane, including confessing some of his past <u>mistakes</u>. This is <u>strange</u> behaviour towards his <u>governess</u>.

4) He wants to <u>marry Jane</u>, despite being much <u>older</u> than her and Jane <u>not</u> being his <u>social equal</u>. He is not concerned about <u>defying</u> social <u>expectations</u>.

5) He dresses up as a <u>gipsy</u> to try and <u>manipulate</u> people — as the gipsy, he tells <u>Blanche</u> that he is <u>not rich</u> and questions <u>Jane</u> about her <u>feelings</u>. This shows how he tries to <u>control</u> people and the lack of <u>respect</u> he has for people's <u>feelings</u> — he <u>doesn't care</u> about <u>upsetting</u> Blanche.

Character Profile — Mr Rochester

Mr Rochester can be deceitful

1) Mr Rochester <u>loves</u> Jane, but he <u>doesn't</u> tell her about his <u>existing wife</u>, and tries to <u>marry</u> Jane <u>without</u> telling her the <u>truth</u>. This makes him seem <u>selfish</u> and <u>dishonest</u>.

2) He pays <u>Grace Poole</u> to look after Bertha and uses her as a <u>scapegoat</u> for all Bertha's strange actions. Grace, and other servants, <u>keep</u> Mr Rochester's <u>secret</u> from Jane.

3) Mr Rochester doesn't <u>reveal</u> his <u>identity</u> to <u>Jane</u> when he first meets her, and he <u>deceives</u> her and his <u>friends</u> when he dresses up as a <u>gipsy</u>. Jane isn't impressed with his deception as the gipsy, calling it a "<u>strange idea</u>" and "<u>scarcely fair</u>".

Writer's Techniques

Brontë presents Mr Rochester as a <u>complex</u> character. He is <u>deceitful</u>, <u>reckless</u> and <u>overbearing</u>, but he is also <u>passionate</u>, <u>protective</u> and <u>perceptive</u>.

He is redeemed by the end of the novel

Background and Context

Mr Rochester's treatment of Bertha seems cruel to <u>modern</u> readers, but the insane were <u>badly treated</u> in the 19th century and <u>asylums</u> were awful places. Mr Rochester <u>argues</u> that he's <u>tried</u> to do the <u>right thing</u> for Bertha by keeping her in "<u>safety and comfort</u>".

1) Mr Rochester's character <u>changes</u> after Jane leaves him, which ultimately <u>enables</u> him to <u>marry</u> her when she returns.

2) He experiences a period of <u>physical</u> and <u>emotional pain</u> during Jane's absence — he <u>loses</u> his <u>eyesight</u> and his <u>left hand</u>, and has a "<u>lonely, hopeless</u>" life without her.

3) However, while he's <u>physically weak</u>, he becomes <u>morally stronger</u>. When Jane finds him at Ferndean, he's no longer interested in "<u>fine clothes</u> and <u>jewels</u>" and offers "<u>very sincere</u>" <u>prayers</u> of <u>repentance</u>.

4) This new <u>humility</u> allows Mr Rochester's marriage to Jane to <u>succeed</u> — he is now <u>capable</u> of the <u>equality</u> in their relationship that Jane always desired, but wouldn't have experienced had they married <u>earlier</u>.

5) <u>Two years later</u>, he <u>regains</u> sight in <u>one eye</u> — this could be a <u>symbol</u> of <u>God's forgiveness</u> for his past <u>sins</u> and a <u>reward</u> for his reformed character. He has achieved a kind of <u>redemption</u>.

Mr Rochester can be seen as a Byronic hero

1) The term '<u>Byronic hero</u>' takes its name from the <u>extravagant</u> early 19th-century <u>poet</u>, <u>Lord Byron</u>.

2) Byronic heroes are usually <u>moody</u>, <u>flawed</u>, <u>mysterious</u>, <u>passionate</u> men, who are <u>sexually desirable</u> and act <u>heroically</u> at some point.

3) Mr Rochester fits <u>most</u> of these terms — he's <u>unpredictable</u>, loves Jane <u>passionately</u>, is <u>haunted</u> by his past and tries to <u>rescue</u> Bertha.

4) However, he's not <u>sexually desirable</u> in the traditional sense, meaning he <u>doesn't exactly</u> fit the description of a Byronic hero. Jane <u>loves</u> him, but she doesn't think he's <u>handsome</u>, and Blanche Ingram is more <u>attracted</u> to his <u>money</u> than to his appearance.

© AF archive/Alamy

Write about the different aspects of Rochester's character...

Personally, I don't know what Jane sees in this mysterious, mopey, moody muppet, but I guess he does have some redeeming features. Show the examiner you understand the complexities of Mr Rochester's character.

Character Profile — St. John Rivers

St. John Rivers — not an actual saint, and bizarrely you pronounce his name 'Sin-jun'.

St. John has dedicated his life to God

1) St. John Rivers is a country <u>clergyman</u> who <u>rescues Jane</u> when she is close to death. Along with his <u>sisters</u>, <u>Diana</u> and <u>Mary</u>, he helps her to <u>recover</u> and then finds her work as a <u>teacher</u>.

2) He tells Jane that he felt "miserable" before he decided to serve God as a <u>missionary</u> — he's now completely <u>committed</u> to going to <u>India</u> and believes that only <u>serving God</u> can make him truly <u>happy</u>.

St. John is...

Handsome: "tall, fair, with blue eyes, and a Grecian profile."

Single-minded: "an austere and despotic nature".

Religious: "Firm, faithful and devoted; full of energy, and zeal, and truth, he labours for his race".

Theme — Religion

In 19th-century Britain, many people believed <u>Christianity</u> was the only 'true' <u>religion</u>. It was seen as <u>noble</u> and '<u>right</u>' to try and <u>convert</u> people overseas.

3) St. John's <u>unswerving faith</u> drives all of his <u>decisions</u>. He's in love with the beautiful <u>Miss Oliver</u>, but he doesn't <u>pursue</u> her because she wouldn't make a good <u>missionary's wife</u>.

4) He is willing to <u>deny</u> himself <u>pleasures</u> on Earth (e.g. the love of Miss Oliver) because they will <u>fade away</u>, whereas loving and serving <u>God</u> wholeheartedly will give him <u>eternal</u> happiness and satisfaction.

He acts as a foil to Mr Rochester

A foil is a character who's presented as a contrast to another character.

1) St. John's wish to make Jane his wife for <u>practical</u> reasons <u>contrasts</u> strongly with Mr Rochester's <u>passionate desire</u> to marry Jane. Mr Rochester even suggests Jane could be his <u>mistress</u> — something that St. John would <u>disapprove</u> of.

2) St. John tells Jane that he's a "<u>cold, hard man</u>" and when he <u>doesn't enjoy Christmas</u> at Moor House, Jane <u>realises</u> he's telling the <u>truth</u>. This contrasts with Mr Rochester's love of parties and socialising.

Character — Jane

St. John can also be seen as a <u>foil</u> to <u>Jane</u> — when he says "I am <u>cold</u>", she replies with "I am <u>hot</u>, and <u>fire</u> dissolves <u>ice</u>". Although they hold similar <u>morals</u> and both live by their <u>principles</u>, Jane and St. John have <u>contrasting personalities</u>.

3) His lack of <u>emotional passion</u> drives Jane's return to Mr Rochester. St John's passion is serving <u>God</u>, and Jane's not prepared to be in a <u>loveless marriage</u>.

St. John's words end the novel

1) St. John is an <u>admirable</u> character — he <u>sticks</u> rigidly to what he believes is <u>right</u>, and is faithful to God.

2) Brontë <u>ends</u> the novel with St. John's <u>last words</u> to Jane, where he speaks about his <u>death</u>. Jane believes he should be <u>admired</u> — even though she didn't want to be his <u>wife</u>, she <u>loves</u> him like a <u>brother</u>.

© Moviestore collection Ltd/Alamy

KEY QUOTE

"Know me to be what I am — a cold, hard man."

St. John is a devoted, religious man whose crucial act of kindness saves Jane's life. To most of us, he seems crazy for not going after the lovely, beautiful Miss Oliver, but Brontë suggests he should be admired for it.

Character Profile — Bertha Mason & Grace Poole

Jane only meets Bertha once, but she's a character who makes a pretty significant impact on the plot.

Bertha is Mr Rochester's wife

1) Bertha is a <u>mysterious character</u> who is kept <u>secret</u> from the reader and Jane for a large part of the novel. Even after she's <u>revealed</u>, the reader still can't be <u>sure</u> of the <u>truth</u> about Bertha's character.

2) The reader does know that she's unpredictable and can be violent — in addition to all the <u>strange laughs</u> and <u>noises</u>, Bertha sets <u>fire</u> to Mr Rochester's <u>bed</u>, <u>attacks Mr Mason</u> (her brother) and <u>rips</u> Jane's <u>bridal veil</u> in the night.

> **Bertha is...**
>
> **Savage**: "it snatched and growled like some strange wild animal"
>
> **Dangerous**: "laid her teeth to his cheek".
>
> **Exotic**: "a fine woman ... tall, dark, and majestic."

Bertha's story is only told from Rochester's viewpoint

Bertha is an outsider — see p.50.

1) Bertha is <u>described</u> as being "<u>mad</u>" and she is clearly <u>dangerous</u> — she badly <u>injures</u> Mr Mason and tries to <u>bite</u> Mr Rochester.

2) Jane is <u>scared</u> of <u>Grace</u> before she knows about <u>Bertha</u>, and when she sees Bertha, she describes her as a "<u>maniac</u>" and a "<u>lunatic</u>".

3) Bertha <u>doesn't appear</u> much and doesn't <u>speak</u> — the reader has to <u>trust</u> Mr Rochester's <u>account</u> of her story. He says she was very <u>beautiful</u>, but that after they got married she was "<u>intemperate and unchaste</u>" (liked to drink lots and slept around), and then went <u>mad</u>.

> **Character — Jane**
>
> Bertha is a <u>foil</u> to Jane — physically she's a "<u>big woman</u>" compared with "<u>little</u>" <u>Jane</u>. They also seem to have very different <u>temperaments</u> — Mr Rochester says he couldn't pass "a <u>single hour</u> of the day" with Bertha, but he <u>loves</u> spending time with Jane.

> **Theme — Marriage**
>
> Mr Rochester's <u>marriage</u> was <u>arranged</u> to Bertha because her family was <u>rich</u>. The <u>failure</u> of their marriage is a clear argument <u>against</u> marrying for <u>money</u>.

4) Mr Rochester <u>claims</u> that Bertha's <u>madness</u> runs in her <u>family</u> and that his father and brother knew of Bertha's mother's insanity before he married Bertha. He presents himself as a <u>victim</u> of their <u>greed</u>.

5) Despite her madness, <u>Bertha</u> is clearly <u>cunning</u> — she manages to <u>escape</u> from her room more than once.

Grace Poole is the scapegoat for Bertha's actions

1) <u>Grace Poole</u> was <u>hired</u> by Mr Rochester to look after Bertha and <u>keep</u> his <u>secret</u> by taking the blame for her actions. She used to work at the "Grimsby retreat" (probably an <u>asylum</u>), but is now <u>well-paid</u> at <u>Thornfield</u>.

2) She sometimes gets <u>drunk</u>, which allows <u>Bertha</u> to <u>escape</u>.

3) Jane <u>can't understand</u> why Grace is kept on as a servant — her <u>presence</u>, and Mr Rochester's <u>reluctance</u> to <u>sack</u> her, creates <u>mystery</u>.

> **Writer's Techniques**
>
> Blaming <u>unnatural events</u> on an <u>ordinary</u> servant like Grace builds <u>tension</u>. The reader <u>suspects</u> that <u>something else</u> is responsible.

4) To an extent, Grace is <u>controlled</u> by <u>Mr Rochester</u> — she must <u>do</u> what he <u>says</u> and take the <u>blame</u> for what Bertha does because she is <u>paid</u> so much by him.

KEY QUOTE

"it snatched and growled like some strange wild animal"

Bertha's described as a bit of a monster, but I reckon I'd have gone mad too if I was her — being taken by my husband from sunny Jamaica to a locked room in England doesn't sound like a dream marriage to me.

Character Profile — Mrs Reed & Children

The Reed family are pretty unfriendly characters — Jane certainly isn't sad to see the back of them.

Mrs Reed is a bitter widow

© BBC FILMS / THE KOBAL COLLECTION / SPARHAM, LAURIE

Mrs Reed is...

Stern: "Silence! This violence is all most repulsive".
Unhappy: "You were born, I think, to be my torment".
Bitter: "I could not forget your conduct to me, Jane".

1) Mrs Reed is the <u>widow</u> of Jane's <u>uncle</u>. As he was <u>dying</u>, he made her <u>promise</u> she'd look after Jane — she <u>resents this</u>.

2) She sees Jane as a <u>nuisance</u>, and doesn't mind that her <u>children</u> are <u>cruel</u> to Jane.

3) Before leaving for school, Jane speaks <u>frankly</u> to Mrs Reed, saying that she is <u>unkind</u> and has treated her with "<u>miserable cruelty</u>".

Mrs Reed's death shows Jane's maturity

1) As a girl, Jane told Mrs Reed that she would <u>never</u> call her "<u>aunt</u>" again, but when she <u>returns</u> to Gateshead to see the <u>dying</u> Mrs Reed, she describes the "flame of <u>resentment</u>" as being "<u>extinguished</u>".

2) Jane has <u>learnt</u> from <u>Helen Burns</u> and decides to <u>forgive</u> Mrs Reed for what happened to her as a <u>child</u>.

3) Mrs Reed <u>regrets</u> telling Jane's <u>uncle</u> that Jane was <u>dead</u>, but only because it's a "<u>torment</u>" to her in her dying moments. She's still <u>bothered</u> by Jane's <u>outburst</u> as a child and not interested in accepting her <u>forgiveness</u>.

4) Jane feels <u>sympathy</u> for Mrs Reed as she <u>dies</u> with so much <u>hatred</u>, calling her a "<u>Poor, suffering</u> woman!".

The fortunes of the Reed children contrast with Jane

1) <u>John</u>, <u>Eliza</u> and <u>Georgiana</u> have a <u>better start</u> in life than Jane, but they all <u>end up</u> being <u>unhappy</u>.

2) There is an <u>ironic</u> change of <u>fortunes</u> for the Reeds <u>compared</u> with Jane. Their family <u>falls apart</u> as Jane finds a <u>new</u> family, and they end up nearly <u>bankrupt</u> as Jane ends up as a <u>rich</u> woman.

3) Jane doesn't <u>admire</u> their <u>life choices</u>, and <u>doesn't mention</u> her cousins again after returning to <u>Thornfield</u>.

John

- John is a <u>selfish bully</u> — he <u>torments</u> Jane at Gateshead and tells her she "ought to <u>beg</u>" rather than live with them.
- He <u>wastes</u> the family's <u>money</u> living a <u>wild</u> life with the "<u>worst</u> men" before committing <u>suicide</u>.

Eliza

- Eliza is a <u>boring</u>, <u>diligent</u> character. She <u>hates Georgiana</u> and <u>broke up</u> her <u>relationship</u> with a <u>lord</u> out of <u>jealousy</u>.
- She goes off to be a <u>nun</u>, which Jane describes as being "<u>walled up alive</u>".

Georgiana

- According to Eliza, Georgiana is "<u>vain</u>" and "<u>absurd</u>". She's also <u>selfish</u>, <u>lazy</u> and <u>needy</u>.
- Georgiana <u>marries</u> a "wealthy, <u>worn-out</u> man of fashion", suggesting she's marrying for <u>money</u> not <u>love</u>.

KEY QUOTE

"I approached my cheek to her lips: she would not touch it."

Mrs Reed's bitterness is quite remarkable — despite knowing that she's treated Jane badly, she refuses to apologise and doesn't seem to want or accept Jane's forgiveness. Her children aren't much better either.

Section Three — Characters

Character Profile — Mrs Fairfax & Adèle Varens

Mrs Fairfax and Adèle both live at Thornfield — now that I think about it, that's about all they've got in common.

Mrs Fairfax is the voice of convention

1) Mrs Fairfax is the <u>housekeeper</u> at <u>Thornfield</u> — she's a <u>steady</u> character who <u>behaves</u> in line with <u>social convention</u>.

2) She's <u>kind</u> to Jane when Jane arrives at Thornfield, and <u>helps</u> her to deal with the <u>social formalities</u> when Rochester's guests are present.

3) However, she's <u>not</u> very <u>inquisitive</u> and only gives Jane <u>minimal</u> information when she asks about other characters — this is very <u>different</u> to Jane's character.

© BBC FILMS / THE KOBAL COLLECTION

Mrs Fairfax is...

Straightforward: "My employer is always civil, and I expect nothing more."

Conventional: "Gentlemen in his station are not accustomed to marry their governesses."

Kind: "I'll tell you how to manage so as to avoid the embarrassment of making a formal entrance".

4) She strongly <u>disapproves</u> of Mr Rochester <u>marrying</u> Jane and tells her to "keep Mr Rochester at a <u>distance</u>". She is <u>sceptical</u> that Mr Rochester is marrying her for <u>love</u>, and is the only voice in the novel that <u>predicts</u> that the <u>marriage</u> will <u>not work</u>.

Adèle Varens is mostly used as a plot device

Foreign characters don't have a particularly positive image in the novel — see p.50.

1) Adèle is the <u>illegitimate daughter</u> of <u>Céline Varens</u>, a <u>French dancer</u>. <u>Mr Rochester</u> had an <u>affair</u> with Céline, but <u>doesn't</u> think he's Adèle's <u>father</u>.

2) A <u>child</u> was called 'illegitimate' if its parents <u>weren't married</u> to each other. Illegitimate children were considered <u>second-class citizens</u> in the 19th century.

3) Mr Rochester brought Adèle to <u>England</u> to give her a <u>better life</u>, and to try and do some <u>good</u> after having a <u>sinful</u>, <u>selfish lifestyle</u>.

Character — Mr Rochester

<u>Mr Rochester</u> often gets frustrated with Adèle, but he does seem to care for her. He brought her <u>home</u> when most 19th-century men wouldn't have done, and this <u>helps</u> the reader to believe him when he claims that he's done the <u>right thing</u> for <u>Bertha</u>.

4) Adèle is <u>vain</u> and <u>silly</u>. She is a <u>caricature</u> (a character with some <u>exaggerated personality traits</u>) of stereotypical <u>French women</u> at the time, who liked <u>gifts</u> and fancy <u>possessions</u>.

5) She <u>doesn't do much</u> in the novel, and Brontë mostly uses her as a <u>plot device</u> (something that <u>drives</u> the plot <u>forwards</u>). Adèle is the <u>reason</u> that <u>Jane</u> comes to <u>Thornfield</u>, and she <u>reveals things</u> about other <u>characters</u>:

- <u>Blanche</u> appears as <u>impatient</u> and <u>snobbish</u> — she calls Adèle a "<u>tiresome monkey</u>".
- Jane's <u>compassion</u> is revealed — she says that Adèle <u>shouldn't pay</u> for the <u>sins</u> of her <u>parents</u>, and continues to <u>look after</u> her regardless of her <u>illegitimate status</u>.

EXAM TIP

Adèle and Mrs Fairfax are both useful characters...

These two aren't the most exciting characters, but Brontë uses them to explore social expectations and to move the plot forwards. Adèle is also handy for revealing things about Jane, Mr Rochester and Blanche.

Character Profile — Mr Brocklehurst & Helen Burns

Two contrasting characters to have a look at here — a cruel clergyman and a sickly schoolgirl.

Mr Brocklehurst is hypocritical

1) Jane describes <u>Mr Brocklehurst</u> as a "<u>black pillar</u>" with a face "like a <u>carved</u> mask"— he's described like a <u>stone</u>, reflecting his <u>cold</u>, imposing <u>nature</u>.

2) He is <u>miserly</u> — he tries to run Lowood on as <u>little money</u> as possible, and <u>challenges</u> Miss Temple whenever he sees that <u>more money</u> has been spent.

3) <u>Many</u> of the girls at Lowood <u>die</u> of <u>typhus</u>, suggesting that the <u>conditions</u> Mr Brocklehurst imposes are too <u>harsh</u>.

> **Mr Brocklehurst is...**
>
> **Hypocritical**: "They [*his daughters*] ought to have come a little sooner to have heard his lecture on dress".
>
> **Uncaring**: "my plan in bringing up these girls is... to render them hardy, patient, self-denying".
>
> **Miserly**: "a lunch ... of bread and cheese, has twice been served ... How is this?"

Copyright © BBC Photo Library

4) He has a <u>rigid</u> view of <u>Christianity</u> and is quick to <u>judge</u> people — he tells Jane she has a "<u>wicked heart</u>" just because she doesn't like reading the <u>Psalms</u>.

5) Brontë <u>exposes</u> him as a <u>hypocrite</u> when his wife and daughters appear at Lowood. They are "<u>splendidly attired</u>" and have "<u>elaborately curled</u>" hair, but Mr Brocklehurst had just ordered that pupils' "<u>top-knots</u> [*a kind of hair bun*] must be <u>cut off</u>."

Helen Burns has a strong influence on Jane

1) When they first <u>meet</u>, Helen is the <u>opposite</u> of Jane — she is <u>badly treated</u> by one of the teachers at Lowood, but she <u>never complains</u> and Jane <u>can't understand</u> this.

2) She is <u>patient</u> and <u>calm</u>, and <u>encourages Jane</u> to be the same. Jane <u>looks up</u> to her and is "struck with <u>wonder</u>" when she <u>listens</u> to Helen talking to <u>Miss Temple</u>.

3) Helen is <u>passive</u> and <u>accepts</u> what happens to her in life — she has "<u>consumption</u>" (tuberculosis), which is <u>fatal</u>. When she's close to death, she <u>doesn't fight</u> the illness and tells Jane that she is "very <u>happy</u>". Her Christian <u>faith</u> is the reason for this — she is happy to be "going to <u>God</u>" — in this way she is <u>similar</u> to St. John (see p.34).

> **Character — Jane**
>
> In <u>contrast</u> to Helen, <u>Jane</u> refuses to "<u>submit passively</u>" to <u>death</u> when she is wandering the <u>moors</u>. Jane <u>begs</u> "Providence" to "<u>sustain</u> me a <u>little longer</u>" — she's an <u>independent</u> spirit who is assertive and determined.

4) Jane takes on some of Helen's <u>teachings</u> and becomes <u>forgiving</u>, <u>compassionate</u> and <u>patient</u> — she learns from Helen's <u>faith</u> in God.

> **Helen Burns is...**
>
> **Religious**: "I believe; I have faith: I am going to God."
>
> **Patient**: "It is far better to endure patiently a smart which nobody feels but yourself".
>
> **Passive**: "Helen... obeyed the monitor without reply as without delay."

KEY QUOTE *"the grim face at the top was like a carved mask"*
Mr Brocklehurst is a bit like a pantomime villain — he's ugly, cruel and looks ridiculous when his fancy family walk in after a lecture about plainness. Helen Burns is a good influence on Jane, but she dies young.

Character Profile — Bessie & Miss Temple

Jane doesn't speak positively about many people from her childhood, but these two are different.

Copyright © BBC Photo Library

Bessie is kind to Jane at Gateshead

1) Bessie is a <u>servant</u> at Gateshead, and although she's <u>not</u> always <u>kind</u> to Jane, she's much <u>kinder</u> than anyone else. After Jane is shut up in the <u>red-room</u>, she says that "Missis was rather <u>too hard</u>" and calls Jane a "<u>poor child</u>".

2) She <u>recognises</u> that Mrs Reed is <u>cruel</u> to Jane, but <u>can't</u> do anything about it because she's <u>employed</u> by <u>Mrs Reed</u>.

3) She has a "<u>quick temper</u>" that Jane <u>dislikes</u> — "She is always <u>scolding</u> me." But she does <u>care</u> for Jane and they are <u>pleased</u> to <u>see each other</u> when Bessie visits <u>Lowood</u> and Jane returns to <u>Gateshead</u>.

> **Bessie is...**
>
> **Kind:** "When thus gentle, Bessie seemed to me the best, prettiest, kindest being in the world".
>
> **Short-tempered:** "You naughty little thing!"
>
> **Motherly:** "Be sure and take good care of her".

Miss Temple is the opposite of Mr Brocklehurst

> **Miss Temple is...**
>
> **Caring:** "she had been called to a delirious patient in the fever-room."
>
> **Admirable:** "I dared not allow them to remain fasting till dinner-time".
>
> **Just:** "when a criminal is accused, he is always allowed to speak in his own defence."

1) Miss Temple is a <u>kind</u> and <u>caring</u> teacher at Lowood. She does what she can to <u>care</u> for the girls and <u>improve</u> their living <u>conditions</u>, but is <u>restricted</u> by Mr Brocklehurst's <u>meanness</u>.

2) She <u>wants</u> to find out the <u>truth</u> about Jane and <u>writes</u> to Mr Lloyd (the apothecary) to try and <u>clear</u> her <u>name</u>. She cares about <u>justice</u> and doesn't <u>judge</u> Jane like Mr Brocklehurst does.

3) She also <u>helps</u> Jane as she grows up at Lowood — Jane says that she feels <u>calmer</u> and "<u>better regulated</u>" after <u>learning</u> from Miss Temple.

Both are surrogate mothers to Jane

1) '<u>Surrogate</u>' means '<u>substitute</u>', so a 'surrogate mother' is someone who <u>stands in</u> for a <u>real mother</u>.

2) Bessie <u>nurses</u> Jane after her <u>illness</u> at Gateshead and tells her <u>stories</u> — things that a <u>mother</u> might do.

3) When Jane <u>visits</u> Bessie and her family, she describes the "<u>occasional tap or push</u>" that Bessie gives her <u>own children</u> as being "just as she <u>used</u> to <u>give me</u>".

4) When <u>Miss Temple</u> leaves Lowood, Jane <u>describes</u> how she has been a "<u>mother</u>, governess" and "<u>companion</u>" to <u>Jane</u> during her time there.

Jane is desperate to be part of a family — see p.42.

5) However, both Miss Temple and Bessie ultimately <u>fail</u> as mother-figures — Bessie is <u>restricted</u> in what she can do because she's only a <u>servant</u>, and Miss Temple <u>leaves</u> Jane behind when she gets <u>married</u>.

Compare Jane's relationships with these characters...

Jane disliked Bessie's temper and cross remarks, but she remembers her fondly and enjoys being reunited with her later. The novel skips most of Miss Temple's time with Jane, but she has a positive influence on her.

Character Profile — Blanche Ingram, Mary & Diana Rivers

Blanche Ingram may be beautiful, but beauty means very little as far as Brontë is concerned.

Blanche is a conventional aristocratic beauty

1) Jane describes Blanche as being "<u>moulded</u> like a <u>Dian</u>" (a <u>goddess</u>) — she is a <u>beautiful</u> young woman.

2) She would make a <u>conventional</u> wife for Rochester, and they <u>appear</u> to <u>get on</u> well when she's at Thornfield. She comes from a <u>wealthy</u> family and looks "<u>majestic</u>".

3) However, Jane sees that Blanche <u>doesn't</u> really <u>please</u> Mr Rochester — the "<u>Arrows</u>" that Blanche "<u>fires</u>" at him <u>bounce</u> off his "breast" and fall "<u>harmless at his feet</u>".

4) Blanche is also <u>snobbish</u> and <u>rude</u>. She <u>shows off</u> her <u>knowledge</u> and is deliberately <u>rude</u> about <u>governesses</u> in front of Jane, calling them "<u>detestable</u>" and "<u>ridiculous</u>".

5) Her <u>shallow</u> nature is exposed by Mr Rochester when he's disguised as a <u>gipsy</u> — the "<u>gipsy</u>" tells her that Rochester is <u>not</u> very <u>rich</u> and she <u>loses interest</u> in <u>marrying</u> him.

© AF archive/Alamy

Writer's Techniques

Blanche's presence <u>foreshadows</u> the <u>revelation</u> about <u>Bertha</u> (see p.55) — Blanche is the <u>first barrier</u> between <u>Jane</u> and <u>Rochester</u>.

Blanche is...

Aristocratic: "the three most distinguished... were the Dowager Lady Ingram and her daughters".
Snobbish: "the haughty voice of Blanche".
Shallow: "I know she considers the Rochester estate eligible to the last degree".

Diana and Mary are Jane's kind cousins

1) Jane is <u>absorbed</u> by Diana and Mary's <u>conversation</u> and "<u>intelligence</u>" when she watches them through the <u>window</u> at Moor House.

2) They are <u>compassionate</u> to Jane when St. John brings her into the house — they <u>nurse</u> her, <u>wash</u> her clothes and give her <u>food</u>.

3) Jane is <u>happy</u> to learn that Diana and Mary are her <u>cousins</u> — the <u>inheritance</u> she shares with them <u>frees</u> them from being <u>governesses</u>.

4) There are <u>similarities</u> between Jane, Diana and Mary:

- They love <u>learning</u> and spend time working as <u>governesses</u>.
- They have no <u>parents</u>, and have no choice but to <u>work</u>.
- <u>Diana agrees</u> with Jane's <u>decision</u> not to go marry <u>St. John</u>.
- All three end up in <u>happy marriages</u>.

Diana and Mary are...

Kind: "Never once in their dialogues did I hear a syllable of regret at the hospitality".

Educated: "she read something, of which not one word was intelligible to me; for it was in an unknown tongue".

Perceptive: "She [Jane] is not an uneducated person, I should think, by her manner of speaking".

KEY QUOTE

"both possessed faces full of distinction and intelligence"

Jane looks longingly through the window at the women of Moor House, and it turns out she's similar to them. Blanche provides a contrast — she wants to marry Mr Rochester for money, but she ends up disappointed.

Practice Questions

Time for some more questions — I know you've been waiting for them. There are lots of important characters in the novel, so this page will check if you know your Bessie from your Blanche and your Rochester from your Rivers.

Quick Questions

1) Give two examples of times when Jane is treated as an outsider.

2) Who does Jane think Mr Rochester is going to marry?

3) What does Grace Poole do that enables Bertha to escape?

4) Give one way in which Mr Brocklehurst is hypocritical.

5) Match the people below to the places they live:
   - a) Mrs Fairfax
   - b) Mrs Reed
   - c) Miss Temple
   - i) Lowood
   - ii) Thornfield
   - iii) Gateshead

6) Which three of the characters below are Jane's cousins?
   - a) St. John   b) Helen   c) Georgiana   d) Diana   e) Bessie

In-depth Questions

1) Describe Jane's character, using quotes to back up your answer.

2) Explain how Mr Rochester achieves redemption by the end of the novel.

3) Do you think St. John Rivers is really a "cold, hard man"?
   Give examples from the text to support your answer.

4) Explain Adèle's role in the novel.

5) What impact does Helen Burns have on Jane's character development?

6) "her friendship and society had been my continual solace; she had stood me in the stead of mother, governess, and latterly, companion."
   Use this quotation to help you describe Jane's feelings towards Miss Temple.

7) Describe Blanche Ingram's character. Use her reaction to the fortune-teller's visit as a starting point.

Practice Questions

That's the starter polished off, now it's time for the main course*. Here are some exam-style questions that will really test whether you've been paying attention. They're great preparation for the questions you'll have to tackle on the big day, so answer them just as if an examiner was going to be reading them.

Exam-style Questions

1) Read this extract, in which Mr Rochester and Jane are talking the morning after Mr Mason has been attacked.

> "Jane, will you have a flower?"
> He gathered a half-blown rose, the first on the bush, and offered it to me.
> "Thank you, sir."
> "Do you like this sunrise, Jane? That sky with its high and light clouds which are sure to melt away as the day waxes warm — this placid and balmy atmosphere?"
> "I do, very much."
> "You have passed a strange night, Jane."
> "Yes, sir."
> "And it has made you look pale — were you afraid when I left you alone with Mason?"
> "I was afraid of someone coming out of the inner room."
> "But I had fastened the door — I had the key in my pocket: I should have been a careless shepherd if I had left a lamb — my pet lamb — so near a wolf's den, unguarded: you were safe."
> "Will Grace Poole live here still, sir?"
> "Oh yes! don't trouble your head about her — put the thing out of your thoughts."
> "Yet it seems to me your life is hardly secure while she stays."
> "Never fear — I will take care of myself."
> "Is the danger you apprehended last night gone by now, sir?"
> "I cannot vouch for that till Mason is out of England: nor even then. To live, for me, Jane, is to stand on a crater-crust which may crack and spew fire any day."
> "But Mr Mason seems a man easily led. Your influence, sir, is evidently potent with him: he will never set you at defiance or wilfully injure you."
> "Oh, no! Mason will not defy me; nor, knowing it, will he hurt me — but, unintentionally, he might in a moment, by one careless word, deprive me, if not of life, yet for ever of happiness."

Starting with this passage, write about how the character of Mr Rochester is presented by Brontë. Write about:
a) how Brontë presents Mr Rochester in this extract
b) how Brontë presents Mr Rochester in the novel as a whole

2) Write about how Brontë presents the changing relationship between Jane and Mr Rochester in the novel.

3) Explore how Charlotte Brontë presents the important decisions Jane has to make. What does this show us about Jane's character?

* Dessert not included.

Section Three — Characters

Marriage

Mr Rochester and St. John both propose to Jane — but their reasons for doing so are very different...

Marriages were often for money or social status

The theme of marriage is one of the ways in which 'Jane Eyre' fits into the romance genre — see p.59.

The plot of *Jane Eyre* focuses on the <u>romantic relationship</u> between Jane and Mr Rochester, but Brontë explores the theme of marriage through <u>other relationships</u> too:

Blanche Ingram and Mr Rochester

People <u>expect</u> Mr Rochester to marry Blanche, because it's a "<u>suitable</u>" match — they're both from similar backgrounds. Blanche Ingram is <u>beautiful</u> and comes from a <u>respectable</u> family. She wants to marry Mr Rochester because he's <u>upper class</u> and <u>wealthy</u>, but he proposes to <u>Jane</u> instead.

Bertha Mason and Mr Rochester

Mr Rochester's family <u>arranged</u> his marriage to Bertha for <u>money</u>, and it <u>ruined his life</u> — even before she went mad. He says he couldn't talk to Bertha because her mind was "common, low, narrow". Brontë suggests that a marriage based on <u>money</u> won't be successful.

Copyright © BBC Photo Library

Rosamund Oliver and St. John Rivers

St. John doesn't marry <u>rich</u> Miss Oliver (who he <u>loves</u>) because he doesn't think she'd be a good missionary's wife — he thinks it's not <u>God's will</u>. He proposes to <u>Jane</u> instead, "for my Saviour's service", even though he admits he <u>doesn't love</u> her. Jane almost <u>agrees</u>, but in the end her <u>passion</u> leads her back to <u>Mr Rochester</u>.

'Jane Eyre' promotes marriages where the couple are equal

1) During the <u>early 19th century</u>, women were often considered to be <u>inferior</u> to men in many ways.

2) When Jane and Mr Rochester are finally able to marry, they are <u>equals</u> — <u>financially</u>, <u>morally</u> and intellectually. Jane has inherited <u>money</u>, and Mr Rochester has <u>repented</u> and been <u>punished</u> for his sins.

3) When <u>Miss Temple</u> gets married, Jane says that her husband is "<u>almost worthy</u> of such a wife", which is an <u>unusual</u> view for a woman to have had at that time — it suggests that Jane thinks women should marry their <u>equal</u>.

4) Diana, Mary and Jane all have <u>happy marriages</u>. They marry for <u>love</u>, and Jane describes her marriage to Mr Rochester as <u>well-balanced</u> — "I am my husband's life as fully as he is mine."

Character — St. John

Jane <u>refuses</u> to marry St. John because they don't <u>love</u> each other and so there would be no chance of any <u>equality</u> — "such a martyrdom would be <u>monstrous</u>". St. John wants to marry Jane for practical reasons — she'd be a good <u>missionary's wife</u>.

KEY QUOTE

"precisely suited in character — perfect concord"

Jane and Mr Rochester are on the same page for a lot of matters (like this Marriage page) so they make a great couple. Who else would be brave enough to honestly tell Mr Rochester just how rough he looks?

Family

It's not just romantic love that plays a part in the novel — family love crops up a lot too.

Jane longs for a loving family

1) Jane lives with <u>relatives</u> at the beginning of the novel, but she's an orphan and isn't treated kindly — she's considered a <u>troublesome</u> "<u>dependant</u>".

2) Throughout the novel, Jane looks for <u>familial love</u> in different places:

- <u>Bessie</u>, a servant at Gateshead; <u>Miss Temple</u>, her teacher; and <u>Mrs Fairfax</u> all act as 'surrogate mothers' to Jane (see p.39). Jane also acts as a kind of surrogate mother to <u>Adèle Varens</u>.
- At <u>school</u>, Jane wants <u>affection</u> — she tells Helen Burns that she would have the "bone of my arm <u>broken</u>" to gain "real affection" from someone she <u>loves</u>.

Jane finds a loving family

1) When Jane leaves Thornfield she has <u>no one</u> to turn to. The Rivers siblings find this <u>surprising</u> — St. John calls it "A most singular position".

© Focus/Everett/REX

2) When Jane discovers that she's <u>related</u> to St. John, Diana and Mary, she's <u>overjoyed</u> and mentions her "<u>craving</u>... for fraternal and sisterly <u>love</u>."

3) At the end of the novel, Jane and Mr Rochester are still <u>happy</u> after ten years, and have a <u>son</u>. <u>Adèle</u> is Jane's friend, and they still see the <u>Rivers sisters</u>.

Writer's Techniques

Brontë presents the Rivers siblings in <u>contrast</u> with the Reed siblings. They're all Jane's <u>cousins</u>, and from <u>respectable</u> families, but they're <u>opposites</u> in <u>character</u>. When the Rivers family <u>replace</u> the Reeds in Jane's life, it shows how Jane's life is <u>getting better</u>, and she ends up with her <u>own</u> family.

The novel highlights family problems

1) The Eyres are related to the Reed and the Rivers families, but they're <u>estranged</u> — the Reeds <u>don't approve</u> of the Eyres, and the Rivers and Eyre families have had a <u>disagreement</u> over money.

2) The Reeds are a <u>dysfunctional</u> family — John commits suicide and Eliza says she will <u>never</u> see Georgiana again after their mother's death.

Theme — Morality

Jane understands that <u>Adèle</u> shouldn't be punished for her <u>parents' mistakes</u>.

3) St. John loves his family — but he loves <u>God</u> more. He is prepared to <u>abandon</u> his sisters and go to <u>India</u> to work as a <u>missionary</u>.

4) Adèle was <u>abandoned</u> by her mother and doesn't know who her father is. This makes Jane more <u>determined</u> to take care of her — she <u>understands</u> what it's like to have no parents.

5) Mr Rochester's family <u>ruined his life</u> by pushing him to <u>marry</u> Bertha.

EXAM TIP

Mention how Jane's family situation gradually gets better...

At the start of the novel, Jane has nobody to love — the closest thing she has to a mother is a crabby maid *sob*. But she gradually finds more stand-in relatives — and then even some real ones. Hurrah!

Religion

Some people say *Jane Eyre* is as much about religion as it is about love — in a way, Jane is torn between them.

Jane meets different types of religious people

Mr Rochester becomes more religious when he loses Jane — this change of attitude is rewarded by Jane's return.

Most of the characters in the novel are <u>religious</u> — religion played a <u>key part</u> in people's lives at the time.

Mr Brocklehurst

* Mr Brocklehurst claims his school is run on <u>Christian principles</u>. However, he treats the pupils in an <u>unchristian</u> way — they're <u>underfed</u> and live in <u>cold</u>, <u>unsanitary</u> conditions. He's also a <u>hypocrite</u> — he orders one girl's natural <u>curls</u> to be cut off, but his <u>daughters</u> have "elaborate curled" hair.

* He uses religion to <u>justify</u> the bad treatment, but it just makes him sound <u>cruel</u> and <u>heartless</u> — e.g. he tells Miss Temple to remind the girls of the "<u>torments of martyrs</u>" in early Christianity, if their porridge is burnt again.

Helen Burns

* Helen is <u>patiently</u> waiting to go to Heaven. She <u>turns the other cheek</u> if anyone hurts her — it's all part of God's plan. Jane <u>admires</u> her faith, and learns from her (she forgives Mrs Reed), but can't change her <u>passionate personality</u>.

* Helen Burns acts as a <u>foil</u> to Jane. Her <u>acceptance</u> and <u>tolerance</u> is a sharp <u>contrast</u> to Jane's <u>passion</u>.

© Snap Stills/REX

St. John Rivers

* St. John wants to <u>serve</u> God completely — he believes he must <u>sacrifice</u> himself to God by going to India, even though he will probably <u>suffer</u> there. He tries to <u>persuade</u> Jane to do the same.

* Jane <u>admires</u> St. John's <u>dedication</u>, but she realises he's rejected human <u>emotions</u> in order to give his whole <u>self</u> to God. She also feels that he hasn't found "that <u>peace</u> of God" she saw in <u>Helen</u>.

Jane is religious in her own way

1) As a <u>child</u>, Jane says to avoid hell she "must keep in <u>good health</u>, and <u>not die</u>" — it's not very Christian.

2) However, as Jane grows up, her <u>faith</u> in God develops, and she tries hard to live in a 'good' and moral way — e.g. she refuses to be Mr Rochester's mistress.

3) Jane's religious <u>journey</u> is a big part of her journey of <u>self discovery</u> — she has a very <u>real</u> religious <u>faith</u>:

* When wandering on the moors, she <u>prays</u> to God and <u>trusts</u> that he will "<u>save</u>" both her and Mr Rochester.

* During her first engagement to Mr Rochester, Jane <u>struggles</u> with the fact that she has "made an <u>idol</u>" of him.

4) Jane almost goes to <u>India</u> with St. John — it <u>looks like</u> she's prepared to <u>sacrifice</u> her life and happiness for God. However, she then rejects this <u>ultimate sacrifice</u> and tries to find a way of life that <u>combines</u> personal <u>happiness</u> with <u>devotion</u> to God.

An idol is something that someone worships instead of God.

KEY QUOTE

"the Bible bids us return good for evil"

This is a classic example of Helen's Christian attitude towards life — don't get angry if someone is cruel to you, just let the experience make you a better person (because the Bible says so). That's pretty deep...

Morality

Jane is often torn between what she believes to be right, what society believes is right and being happy.

Mr Rochester's actions seem immoral

1) Mr Rochester <u>doesn't tell</u> Jane about Bertha and <u>lies</u> by blaming strange events on Grace Poole.

2) He almost <u>leads</u> Jane into a <u>bigamous marriage</u> which would have been <u>illegal</u> and <u>immoral</u>.

3) After the marriage is stopped, Mr Rochester wants Jane to be his <u>mistress</u> and live <u>abroad</u>, even though he's already shown <u>regret</u> for having had other <u>mistresses abroad</u>.

> **Character — Mr Rochester**
>
> Mr Rochester doesn't believe Adèle is his daughter, but he still <u>takes care</u> of her. He's trying to <u>make up</u> for his past immoral behaviour — "expiating numerous sins".

4) However, he doesn't believe he's being <u>immoral</u> at the time — his <u>judgement</u> is clouded by his <u>desire</u> to be happy. While Jane <u>sacrifices</u> her happiness to do what she believes is <u>right</u>, Mr Rochester <u>ignores</u> what society says is right, in order to be <u>happy</u>.

5) At the <u>end</u> of the novel Mr Rochester admits he was <u>wrong</u>, and says that if Jane had become his <u>mistress</u>, he would have "sullied my innocent flower".

Jane tries to do the right thing

1) Jane has strong <u>opinions</u> about what's <u>right</u> and <u>wrong</u>, and tries to live by these <u>principles</u>. Eventually, she manages to <u>balance</u> this with her own <u>happiness</u>.

2) As an adult, Jane <u>forgives</u> Aunt Reed even though she made her suffer — she wants her to die in <u>peace</u>.

3) Jane <u>forgives</u> Mr Rochester's lies. However, she "must leave him <u>decidedly</u>, <u>instantly</u>, <u>entirely</u>" because she can't live in <u>sin</u>.

4) Jane doesn't think it's <u>right</u> to <u>marry</u> St. John because she doesn't <u>love</u> him, even though this would have been more <u>socially acceptable</u> than travelling with him as a <u>single woman</u>.

5) Jane immediately decides to <u>share</u> her inheritance <u>equally</u> with the Rivers family — it's what seems <u>fair</u> to her.

Doing the right thing is rewarded

To Brontë, the right thing is not the conventional thing — Mr Rochester's marriage to Blanche would have been conventional, but it wouldn't have made him happy.

1) Mr Rochester is <u>physically hurt</u> to pay for his sins. He looks to God for <u>forgiveness</u>, and is <u>rewarded</u> with Jane's return and with the <u>sight</u> in one of his eyes.

2) The <u>happy ending</u> is a reward for Jane's <u>patience</u> and for her doing the <u>right thing</u> — there are <u>hints</u> that if she'd stayed with Mr Rochester, their relationship would have <u>failed</u> like his other relationships with <u>mistresses</u>.

3) Diana and Mary are <u>respectable</u> characters who support Jane, and they both <u>marry for love</u>.

4) St. John is likely to <u>die in India</u>, but Jane is confident that he will receive his "<u>sure reward</u>" from God for his sacrifice. St. John himself is happy to be going to <u>God</u>.

Don't forget to say how characters change and develop...

Mr Rochester becomes much more bothered about what's right and wrong as the novel develops — that's Jane's good influence for you. Actually, he has to be blind before he can see things clearly — funny that.

Secrecy and Deception

There are all sorts of secrets being kept in *Jane Eyre* — Mr Rochester can be downright sneaky at times. Anyway, the truth will out eventually, and it certainly does in this novel.

There are hints that secrets are being kept

1) Jane describes the attic corridor at Thornfield as being like "Bluebeard's castle" (see p.15), which foreshadows future events in the novel.

2) After the fire in Mr Rochester's bedroom, Jane overhears a servant asking "Doesn't she know?" — Jane knows there's a secret at Thornfield, but she doesn't ask questions about it.

> **Background and Context**
>
> *Jane Eyre* was even surrounded by deception in real life — Brontë used a pseudonym when it was first published (see p.1).

3) The cover-up involving Grace Poole doesn't seem to add up — she's blamed for the strange noises and events, but whenever Jane sees her she's behaving normally.

4) The games Mr Rochester plays with his guests follow the theme of deception — he plays a game of charades in which he and Blanche pretend to get married.

Mr Rochester conceals things

1) Mr Rochester doesn't tell Jane who he is when they first meet — although he asks her who she is.

2) He dresses up as a gipsy so that he can try and manipulate Jane and Blanche.

© Moviestore/REX

3) Mr Rochester pretends to be in love with Blanche to make Jane jealous.

4) He hides Bertha at Thornfield and hides the truth about the strange noises, his marriage and Mr Mason's visit.

5) In the end he loses his sight — things are now hidden from him. His blindness helps him to learn from his mistakes.

6) Jane mirrors Mr Rochester's deception when she visits Ferndean — she hides her identity at first. This suggests that the balance of power has changed.

Many secrets are kept from Jane

1) Mrs Reed doesn't tell Jane she has an uncle for a long time. She also tells him that Jane is dead.

2) Mr Rochester keeps his love for Jane secret — Jane suffers because she believes he wants to marry Blanche. She thinks he's teasing her when he asks her to marry him, so she tells him she isn't "soulless and heartless".

3) The biggest deception is that Mr Rochester is already married, and Jane only finds out at the altar.

4) Even though Jane has things hidden from her, she is usually open and honest both with other characters and with the "reader", who she addresses directly. This makes it easier to understand and trust her point of view. Brontë uses her as narrator for the whole novel, so the reader only finds out what happens when she does.

> **Character — Mr Rochester**
>
> Mr Rochester is also a victim of secrecy — his father and brother didn't tell him that madness runs in Bertha's family.

"there was a mystery at Thornfield..."

If there's one thing I know about Mr Rochester, it's that he loves a good secret — poor old Jane. Mind you, Jane isn't completely truthful 100% of the time — just ask St. John, who knew someone called Jane Elliott...

Gender

Jane Eyre was written by a woman, and it makes a few points about 19th-century gender issues...

19th-century women were seen as inferior to men in some ways

1) <u>Women</u> had few <u>rights</u> in the <u>19th century</u>. They were <u>lower status</u> than, and usually <u>dependent</u> on, men.

2) <u>Marriage</u> was important to women because a husband would <u>support</u> them. Women usually needed to be <u>pretty</u>, <u>rich</u> or from a <u>good family</u> to secure a <u>good marriage</u> — these were the <u>important qualities</u> in the middle and upper classes at the time.

3) The importance of finding a <u>husband</u> is shown by the many <u>female</u> characters whose <u>stories</u> are finished with a marriage — <u>Miss Temple</u> leaves Lowood when she gets married, <u>Miss Oliver</u> gives up on St. John and marries Mr Granby, <u>Georgiana Reed</u> marries a rich older man, and <u>Jane</u>, <u>Diana</u> and <u>Mary</u> all get married.

4) St. John completely <u>refuses</u> to let Jane to travel to India alongside him without them being <u>married</u>. It was rare for a woman to travel abroad on her own — she would normally go as a <u>companion</u> to her husband.

5) Mr Rochester had <u>relationships</u> with women in Europe — but he sees them as "<u>inferior</u>" and the time he spent with them as "<u>degrading</u>".

6) There was a big <u>double standard</u> in society about <u>sex outside marriage</u>. It was considered completely <u>unacceptable</u> for a <u>woman</u> to have sex outside marriage, but <u>men</u> were not <u>judged</u> so <u>harshly</u>.

Bertha could be an oppressed woman

Theme — Madness

In the 19th century, women were often diagnosed as <u>insane</u> or <u>hysterical</u> if they showed <u>immoral</u> or <u>unfeminine</u> behaviour. Many women became <u>depressed</u> or <u>stressed</u> due to their lack of <u>independence</u>.

1) The reader only hears Mr Rochester's <u>account</u> of Bertha's story. He says that even <u>before</u> she went mad, Bertha was "<u>intemperate</u> and <u>unchaste</u>", suggesting she <u>drank</u> lots and slept with other <u>men</u>. This was not how women were <u>expected</u> to behave.

2) If the reader <u>trusts</u> Mr Rochester's account, then Bertha is <u>not oppressed</u> — he has <u>saved</u> her from the <u>asylum</u> and has made sure that she's <u>looked after</u>.

3) However, if Mr Rochester is <u>lying</u>, then Bertha does appear as an <u>oppressed</u> woman. She's been <u>locked away</u> and <u>silenced</u> by her husband, <u>symbolising</u> the lack of <u>freedom</u> for 19th-century wives.

4) Jane feels <u>sorry</u> for Bertha — she's been <u>abandoned</u> by society and Mr Rochester speaks of her "with <u>hate</u>".

Male characters try to dominate Jane

1) <u>John Reed</u>, <u>Mr Brocklehurst</u>, <u>Mr Rochester</u> and <u>St. John</u> all try to <u>control</u> Jane in different ways.

2) John Reed and Mr Brocklehurst <u>bully</u> Jane.

3) Mr Rochester <u>bosses</u> Jane around like a <u>servant</u> at the start of her time at Thornfield ("Go into the library") and only <u>sees</u> her when he <u>feels</u> like it. Even after they become better acquainted, he still tries to maintain <u>control</u> — telling her "<u>Promise me</u> to only stay a week" when she leaves for Gateshead.

4) <u>St. John</u> also orders Jane around, and wants to <u>marry</u> her and take her to India. He wants her to sacrifice herself to help him fulfil his "vocation" and desires.

5) Jane <u>stands up</u> to the male characters in the novel as best she can. She sees herself as <u>at least</u> their <u>equal</u>.

Gender

Gender equality wasn't a thing in Victorian times, so Jane's views would have been very unusual.

There are some unconventional female characters

1) Jane isn't pretty, but she wins Mr Rochester's heart because she's <u>different</u> and <u>intelligent</u>. This is <u>unusual</u> for the 19th century — women were expected to be <u>rich</u>, <u>beautiful</u> or from a <u>good family</u> to find a good husband.

2) Diana and Mary love <u>learning</u> and are <u>kind</u> and <u>intelligent</u>. Jane <u>admires</u> them, and it's clear that they're the kind of women that <u>Brontë approves</u> of too.

© Focus/Everett/REX

3) Bertha is <u>violent</u>, <u>mad</u> and her physical appearance reminds Jane of a "<u>vampire</u>". Mr Rochester calling her "impure, depraved" also suggests that she didn't behave as an <u>upper class woman</u> was expected to do, even before she went <u>mad</u>.

Brontë also comments on masculinity

1) Mr Rochester is described in a very <u>masculine</u> way — Jane says he's "dark, <u>strong</u>, and <u>stern</u>", and he's <u>grumpy</u> and <u>domineering</u>. He <u>isn't handsome</u> and he has features of a Byronic hero (see p.33).

2) Victorian society doesn't really <u>judge</u> Mr Rochester for having <u>mistresses</u>. Brontë <u>highlights</u> the <u>inequalities</u> in society — Jane would definitely be judged if she became Mr Rochester's <u>mistress</u>.

3) Brontë seems to suggest that Mr Rochester <u>needs</u> Jane and shouldn't be <u>blinded</u> by his masculine <u>pride</u>:

- Mr Rochester is used to being <u>obeyed</u> and doesn't often ask for <u>help</u>. However, when he's in <u>trouble</u> he's drawn to Jane — he <u>needs</u> and <u>gets</u> her help when Mr Mason is attacked.

- He asks for Jane's <u>advice</u> when he's considering committing <u>bigamy</u>: "are you <u>justified</u> in overleaping an obstacle of custom...?" But he <u>doesn't listen</u> to Jane's advice, which causes both of them <u>pain</u>.

Jane could be considered a feminist heroine

Feminism is a movement that believes women are completely equal to men.

1) Brontë has created a <u>strong heroine</u> with feminist characteristics. Jane is a woman <u>in charge</u> of her own life — "I am no bird; and no net ensnares me".

2) She's <u>frustrated</u> by the fact that women aren't considered <u>equal</u> to men, and says it's "<u>narrow minded</u>" to expect women to "confine themselves" to trivial activities that society approves of.

3) Jane is Mr Rochester's <u>equal</u> in intelligence.

4) She talks about <u>dreaming</u> of Mr Rochester and "being in his arms" when she's in Morton school house. This is unusual as women didn't openly talk about their <u>physical desires</u> at the time.

5) Jane marries Mr Rochester because it's what <u>she</u> wants. The famous line, "Reader, <u>I</u> married <u>him</u>", shows this — Jane is the <u>active</u> force ("I") in the sentence. The <u>power balance</u> between them is now more <u>even</u>, and may even be tipped in Jane's favour. Mr Rochester is <u>physically</u> and <u>emotionally dependent</u> on her, and Jane now has her <u>own</u> money and family.

KEY QUOTE

"women... suffer from too rigid a restraint"

Jane is reluctant to let anyone or anything control her, and she certainly doesn't follow a man's orders just because he's a man — even if it is Mr Rochester. Even when she marries him, she's not dependent on him.

Foreignness and Outsiders

People are often afraid of what they don't know or understand. This crops up quite a bit in the novel...

There are prejudices towards outsiders

The treatment of Bertha can be seen to symbolise the treatment of foreigners in 19th-century Britain.

1) In the 19th century, people were often <u>prejudiced</u> about <u>foreigners</u> or people who were <u>different</u>.

2) <u>Mr Mason</u> and his sister Bertha, both from Jamaica, are described <u>negatively</u>:

> <u>Jane</u> describes <u>Mr Mason</u> as having an "<u>odd</u>" look" and says his accent is "<u>not altogether English</u>", suggesting he's in some way <u>inferior</u>.

> Bertha's <u>wild</u> physical descriptions reflect <u>19th-century opinions</u> about <u>foreigners</u>. Jane says her face is "<u>purple</u>" and "<u>bloated</u>", and she has "<u>grizzled</u>" hair, <u>wild</u> as a mane".

3) Adèle's <u>irritating</u> traits such as <u>vanity</u> and <u>materialism</u> are put down to her being <u>French</u>. Later, Jane says her English education "corrected in a great measure her French defects".

Bertha is the main outsider

1) The first time Bertha is mentioned, she's described as having a "<u>preternatural</u>" (abnormal and unnatural) laugh.

2) People with <u>mental illnesses</u> were often locked away at the time — there was no attempt to <u>integrate</u> them into <u>society</u>.

3) Some people see <u>Bertha's imprisonment</u> as symbolising the 19th-century fear of "<u>foreignness</u>". Mr Rochester found her personality "<u>totally alien</u>" to his own, right from the start of their marriage.

4) When Jane finally meets <u>Bertha</u>, she's described as a "<u>maniac</u>". Her hair is <u>wild</u> and her face is <u>grotesque</u> — she's completely <u>different</u> from any other character in the book in her <u>looks</u> and <u>behaviour</u>.

Jane is also an outsider

1) As a child, Jane is treated as an <u>outsider</u> — the Reeds <u>don't</u> treat her like <u>family</u>, and most of the servants aren't interested in her.

2) She's treated <u>disrespectfully</u> by some of Mr Rochester's friends because she's a governess and from a <u>lower class</u> than them.

3) When Jane arrives at Moor House, she is outside <u>looking in</u> — she <u>watches</u> Mary and Diana and is <u>attracted</u> to their "delicacy and cultivation." However, Hannah won't let her in at first because she is a poor <u>stranger</u>.

© Focus/Everett/REX

4) She shows <u>compassion</u> for other <u>outsiders</u> — <u>Adèle's</u> past makes her determined to care for her and she says that <u>Bertha</u> "cannot help being mad".

⬤ EXAM TIP *Put the novel into its historical context...*

Jane Eyre is set in the 19th century, when attitudes towards foreigners and mental illness were very different from modern views. Hiding your wife upstairs probably didn't seem as extreme to the novel's first readers.

The Supernatural

There are no actual vampires or werewolves in *Jane Eyre*, but sometimes things get a bit spooky...

There are hints of the supernatural in the novel

1) When Jane first meets Mr Rochester, she is afraid that Pilot is actually a "gytrash" — a supernatural dog.

2) Bertha bites Mr Mason — he's badly injured. Jane also wakes up one night to find Bertha in her room — she says the sight reminded her of a "vampire". These things happen before the reader knows what's locked in the attic, so they build suspense.

3) Just after Jane agrees to marry Mr Rochester, lightning strikes and splits the tree where they had been sitting — this is a bad omen.

© Moviestore Collection/Alamy

4) Jane is influenced by supernatural forces:

- The night before she leaves Thornfield, Jane has a "trance-like dream" in which she sees a "vision" of a "white human" she calls "Mother". The figure tells her to "flee temptation!", which Jane does by leaving Thornfield and Mr Rochester behind.

- As she's wavering between going to India with St. John and staying in England, she hears Mr Rochester's voice calling her. Later he says he had called her name the same evening.

5) As a child, Jane believes the red-room at Gateshead is haunted by her Uncle Reed's ghost, although she admits in hindsight that her imagination got carried away.

6) Mrs Fairfax says that if Thornfield had a ghost, the third-floor "would be its haunt" — it's dark and mysterious.

Brontë uses lots of supernatural language

1) Mr Rochester suggests Jane "bewitched" his horse when they first met, and he often calls her names such as "elf" and "fairy" in an affectionate way. He also describes Jane's paintings as "elfish".

2) Mr Rochester calls Bertha a "demon". Her behaviour could be seen as demonic — lighting fires and ripping Jane's wedding veil.

3) Like many other people in the 19th century, Jane is superstitious:

Jane Eyre has strong Gothic themes (see p.59). During the 19th century, many people were interested in the supernatural. Spooky legends and ghost stories were popular and lots of 'Gothic' novels were written at this time.

- She describes things as being "preternatural" — strange and inexplicable.

- She talks about dreams predicting danger — she "often recalled" Bessie's warning that "to dream of children was a sure sign of trouble".

KEY QUOTE

"She sucked the blood: she said she'd drain my heart"

Jane doesn't know what's happened to Mr Mason, so when he says this she (and the reader) start to believe that there could actually be a blood-sucking vampire living at Thornfield. I told you things got spooky.

Practice Questions

And the theme of the next two pages is... 'Questions'. You know the drill by now — keep your answers to the Quick Questions shot and snappy, but put a little more time and effort into the In-depth questions. If you get stuck, use the pages of Section Four to help you out. Go go go!

Quick Questions

1) Name one character in the novel who marries for money.

2) Name two motherly figures in Jane's life.

3) Give one example of when Jane acts morally.

4) Briefly explain how one character is treated as an outsider.

5) Name a time when Jane feels she is influenced by supernatural forces.

In-depth Questions

1) Explain how Mr Rochester and Jane are an unconventional couple.

2) Compare and contrast Jane's relationships with the Reed and Rivers families.

3) Do you think it's fair to say that Mr Rochester is an immoral character? Explain your answer?

4) Do you think Charlotte Brontë thought it was fair that women were often considered inferior to men? Give reasons for your answer.

Practice Questions

Now for the serious stuff. These questions will give you some proper practice for the exam, so it's worth giving them a go without looking back over the section.

Exam-style Questions

1) Read this extract, where Jane meets Mr Rochester for the first time.

> As this horse approached, and as I watched for it to appear through the dusk, I remembered certain of Bessie's tales, wherein figured a North-of-England spirit called a "Gytrash," which, in the form of horse, mule, or large dog, haunted solitary ways, and sometimes came upon belated travellers, as this horse was now coming upon me.
>
> It was very near, but not yet in sight; when, in addition to the tramp, tramp, I heard a rush under the hedge, and close down by the hazel stems glided a great dog, whose black and white colour made him a distinct object against the trees. It was exactly one form of Bessie's Gytrash—a lion-like creature with long hair and a huge head: it passed me, however, quietly enough; not staying to look up, with strange pretercanine eyes, in my face, as I half expected it would. The horse followed,—a tall steed, and on its back a rider. The man, the human being, broke the spell at once. Nothing ever rode the Gytrash: it was always alone; and goblins, to my notions, though they might tenant the dumb carcasses of beasts, could scarce covet shelter in the commonplace human form. No Gytrash was this,—only a traveller taking the short cut to Millcote. He passed, and I went on; a few steps, and I turned: a sliding sound and an exclamation of "What the deuce is to do now?" and a clattering tumble, arrested my attention. Man and horse were down; they had slipped on the sheet of ice which glazed the causeway. The dog came bounding back, and seeing his master in a predicament, and hearing the horse groan, barked till the evening hills echoed the sound, which was deep in proportion to his magnitude. He snuffed round the prostrate group, and then he ran up to me; it was all he could do,—there was no other help at hand to summon.

Using the extract above as a starting point, discuss how Brontë presents Jane's attitudes towards the supernatural in the novel.

2) How is the theme of 'foreignness and outsiders' used to create mystery in the novel?

3) Jane Eyre can be viewed as an unconventional female character. How does Brontë present her as a strong woman? Remember to write about the society the characters live in.

4) "The fact that Brontë ends the novel with St. John's sacrifice shows that religion is the most important force in Jane's life."
To what extent do you agree with this statement? Use evidence from the text to support your answer.

Narrative and Structure

Time to have a look at how Charlotte Brontë put *Jane Eyre* together, starting with how it's narrated.

The novel is written in the first person

1) Jane is the narrator of the novel. She talks directly to the reader — "Hear an illustration, reader", and gives them detailed information about what she sees and how she feels.

2) The novel was originally published with the subtitle "An Autobiography" — it's a fictional autobiography that follows Jane's life.

3) Some stories and anecdotes are told by other characters. These give the reader interesting and important information they wouldn't otherwise know. They also make the reader feel more engaged, as they hear these things at the same time that Jane does:

- Mr Rochester describes how he ended up being married to Bertha and talks about his travels across Europe.
- St. John tells the story of Jane's uncle and explains how Jane is related to the Rivers.
- An innkeeper tells Jane what happened to Bertha, Mr Rochester and Thornfield in the fire.

Jane seems to be a reliable narrator

1) The reader has to trust that Jane's account is true — only her viewpoint is described in the novel.

2) It's clear that Jane's in charge of the narrative — she chooses the scenes she wants to share and how they appear — "when I draw up the curtain this time, reader". She could exaggerate, make up or omit events without the reader knowing.

3) She skips eight years at Lowood and ten years at Ferndean — she's telling a story rather than writing a comprehensive autobiography — "this is not to be a regular autobiography".

4) Jane writes the account as an adult, so the reader might question how reliable her memory of childhood events is. However, it does mean she's writing with an adult's maturity.

5) Jane's humility also helps the reader to trust her — she calls herself a "fantastic idiot" for believing that Mr Rochester might love her, and she ends the book with St. John's words rather than her own.

The novel is divided into three volumes

1) *Jane Eyre* was originally published in three separate volumes — 19th century readers had to buy or borrow each volume individually to read the whole novel.

2) The first two volumes end on cliffhangers to encourage readers to buy the next volume. Volume One ends after Jane rescues Mr Rochester from the fire, and Volume Two finishes just after Jane finds out about Bertha.

3) The danger at the end of the first volume is a hint about the events to come in Volume Two.

Narrative and Structure

Don't worry, it's a page on structure, but I can confirm that there are zero references to engineering.

The novel is structured by Jane's growth and changes

1) The novel is mostly <u>chronological</u> (moves forwards in time) and covers <u>three</u> major <u>stages</u> in Jane's <u>life</u>:

Jane as a <u>child</u> (aged 10) at <u>Gateshead</u> and <u>Lowood</u> school.	Jane as a <u>young adult</u> (aged 18-20) at <u>Thornfield</u> and <u>Moor House</u>.	Jane as a <u>married mother</u> (aged 30) at <u>Ferndean</u>.

2) It focuses mainly on the <u>two-year period</u> between Jane <u>leaving Lowood</u> and her <u>return</u> to <u>Mr Rochester</u> when he's living at <u>Ferndean</u>.

3) There's an <u>eight-year gap</u> in the novel between <u>Helen's death</u> and <u>Jane's departure</u> from <u>Lowood</u>. Jane <u>claims</u> that these years have <u>no</u> "<u>degree of interest</u>", but she <u>changes significantly</u> during her <u>adolescent years</u>, and the <u>reader</u> has to <u>trust</u> her decision <u>not</u> to include them.

4) After Jane <u>marries</u> Mr Rochester, there's <u>ten-year gap</u> before the <u>end</u> of the book. This is when Jane <u>writes</u> the novel — roughly <u>twelve</u> years after arriving at <u>Thornfield</u> and <u>twenty</u> years after leaving <u>Gateshead</u>.

The novel's themes give it a linear structure

Jane's life generally <u>improves</u> as the novel <u>progresses</u> — she <u>gains</u> a <u>family</u> and money, and becomes a <u>well-educated</u> woman:

Family

Jane begins as a <u>despised orphan</u>, <u>excluded</u> by the Reed <u>family</u>. She becomes a <u>respected</u> member of <u>staff</u> at Thornfield, a <u>beloved cousin</u> at Moor House and finally a <u>wife</u> and <u>mother</u> at Ferndean.

Education

Jane has to <u>read books</u> behind a <u>curtain</u> at Gateshead, but then gets a <u>good education</u> at Lowood, becomes a <u>governess</u> and runs her <u>own school</u> in Morton. The <u>Rivers</u> family also <u>inspire</u> her to learn new things she otherwise wouldn't have.

© iStockphoto.com/naphtalina

Foreshadowing is used as a structural technique

Brontë uses <u>foreshadowing</u> (hinting about events to come) to <u>structure</u> the <u>novel</u>:

- Just after Jane arrives at <u>Thornfield</u>, she hears a "<u>preternatural</u>" (unnatural) <u>laugh</u> — this hints that there's something <u>mysterious</u> hidden in the house, which turns out to be <u>Bertha</u>.

- <u>Blanche Ingram's</u> presence foreshadows Jane learning of <u>Bertha's</u> existence. Blanche is a <u>barrier</u> between Jane and Mr Rochester — "Your <u>bride</u> stands <u>between</u> us." — before Jane meets Mr Rochester's <u>secret wife</u>.

- The <u>lightning</u> that hits the <u>chestnut tree</u> at Thornfield foreshadows the <u>split</u> between Jane and Mr Rochester.

Describe the different ways Brontë structures the novel...

When you write about foreshadowing in the exam, try and mention how Brontë uses it as a structural device. She includes subtle hints throughout the novel that show she's carefully planned what's going on.

Dialogue

There's plenty of dialogue in *Jane Eyre* — Jane always seems to be chatting to someone.

Jane and Mr Rochester's conversations are important

1) Brontë <u>develops</u> Jane and Mr Rochester's <u>relationship</u> through their <u>conversations</u>.

2) At first, Mr Rochester is <u>inquisitive</u> and asks <u>questions</u>, e.g. "Who are your parents?" Jane is also curious — she <u>questions</u> Mrs Fairfax about Mr Rochester: "Do you like him? Is he generally liked?"

© AF archive/Alamy

3) Jane <u>defies</u> convention by <u>answering</u> Mr Rochester without the expected <u>politeness</u>. She answers "<u>No, sir.</u>" when Mr Rochester asks if she thinks he's <u>handsome</u>.

4) As time goes on, Jane <u>warms</u> to Rochester and <u>playfully</u> points out his faults — "You are human and fallible." Their <u>conversation</u> seems to have the <u>equality</u> that Jane wants in their <u>relationship</u>.

5) <u>Mr Rochester</u> becomes more <u>open</u> and stops asking as many <u>questions</u>. He tells Jane about his "<u>numerous sins</u>", even though he knows it's "<u>strange</u>" to discuss such things with someone so "<u>inexperienced</u>".

6) Conversation <u>remains</u> part of their relationship when they are <u>married</u> — "<u>We talk</u>, I believe, <u>all day long</u>".

Characters' personalities are revealed in their dialogue

Brontë uses <u>characters' speech</u> to <u>emphasise</u> points about their <u>personalities</u>:

Helen Burns

When Helen is about to die, her speech is <u>calm</u> and <u>simple</u> — "I believe; I have faith: I am going to God." Her strong <u>faith</u> means she can face death without <u>fear</u>.

St. John Rivers

St. John's <u>devotion</u> to <u>God</u> is revealed further in his speech. He speaks with <u>passion</u> about his <u>mission</u> — "My <u>great work</u>", but <u>coldly</u> about the <u>woman</u> he <u>loves</u> — "She will <u>forget</u> me..."

Adèle Varens

Adèle's <u>materialism</u> is shown through her speech. She <u>pesters</u> Rochester for her <u>present</u> and exclaims "Ma boîte! ma boîte!" ("My box!") when she finally receives it.

Other characters' dialogue also reveals things about Jane

Brontë uses other characters' speech to <u>add</u> to the <u>picture</u> of Jane that the <u>reader</u> gets from <u>Jane</u> herself:

- <u>Mary</u> and <u>Diana</u> Rivers discuss Jane while she's <u>ill</u> in bed. They show how Jane has <u>grown</u> into a <u>sophisticated woman</u>, saying "her <u>accent</u> was <u>quite pure</u>" and that her clothes are "little worn and <u>fine</u>."

- <u>Diana</u> tells Jane: "Plain! You? Not at all." This suggests that Jane may be <u>prettier</u> than she says, and that she might be <u>modest</u> at times.

- <u>Mr Rochester</u> says that Jane is "full of <u>strange contrasts</u>." He gives an <u>honest account</u> of Jane's character — her <u>kind heart</u> and <u>humility</u>, but also the "<u>daring</u>" expression she has when <u>answering</u> him.

- <u>St. John</u> tells Jane the <u>conclusions</u> he's made about her character. He comments on how she works with an "<u>unflagging energy</u>", enjoys the "<u>excitement of sacrifice</u>" and displays an "<u>unshaken temper</u>".

"there was penetration and power in each glance you gave"

Mr Rochester's words give the reader a fuller picture of what Jane is like — it's pretty difficult for her to accurately describe herself all the time. He finds Jane's frankness and lack of flattery a refreshing change.

Setting

Even though *Jane Eyre* is quite a long novel, Brontë still crams in an impressive number of locations.

There are five main settings in 'Jane Eyre'

1) Gateshead, Lowood, Thornfield, Moor House and Ferndean all represent different parts of Jane's life. The names of the places are symbolic — they each reflect Jane's experience there:

- Gateshead — 'gate' shows that this is the start of Jane's journey. Her life moves on from this point.
- Lowood — 'low' reflects the poor conditions at the school and Jane's mistreatment by Mr Brocklehurst.
- Thornfield — 'thorn' suggests that there's something dangerous and hurtful at Mr Rochester's home.
- Moor House — a 'moor' is an open space in the countryside, representing the freedom Jane finds here.
- Ferndean — a 'fern' is a plant. This symbolises new beginnings, life and growth, and ferns traditionally symbolised confidence and shelter.

2) The places also reflect their occupants — Thornfield has Gothic "battlements", making it seem like a fortress and Moor House is "clean and neat" which reflects the Rivers siblings' personalities.

Jane longs for a home

1) Jane is an outsider and is desperate for a 'home'. She isn't wanted at Gateshead, and Lowood feels different after Miss Temple leaves.

2) She tells Mr Rochester that "wherever you are is my home", but Thornfield can't be their home together because of Bertha.

3) She has her own home in Morton, but she isn't truly satisfied there because she misses Mr Rochester.

4) The fact that Thornfield is destroyed in the fire means that Jane and Mr Rochester can create their own home at Ferndean — Jane finally has somewhere she fully belongs.

Writer's Techniques

Lots of important events happen outside — all three marriage proposals and several significant conversations. Nature represents a freedom for characters, away from indoor settings that can be more formal and restrictive.

Jane's journeys between places are significant

1) When Jane is sent alone to Lowood, a servant describes the journey as "a long way!" This emphasises that Jane is all alone in the world.

2) When Jane runs away from Thornfield, she leaves her belongings on the coach. This represents the loss of her last physical link with Thornfield.

3) Her uncle's money makes her journey back to Thornfield much easier, and she is able to offer the innkeeper extra money to get her to Ferndean.

4) However, she finishes the journey on foot and almost gets lost. The money doesn't solve everything — only being reunited with Mr Rochester does that.

Write about Jane's desire for somewhere to call 'home'...

Jane lives in several different places and travels quite a long way in the novel, but it's only at the very end that she can finally settle down. 'Home is where the heart is' — a cheesy cliché, but very true for Jane.

Symbolism

Brontë uses symbols to reinforce the themes that run through the novel.

Fire is an important symbol

1) Fire symbolises <u>warmth</u> and <u>homeliness</u>, but it's also got an <u>element</u> of <u>danger</u> to it.

2) At <u>Lowood</u>, Jane <u>struggles</u> to get near the <u>fire</u> because of the "<u>double row</u> of great girls" who surround it. She doesn't feel at <u>home</u> there, and the <u>atmosphere</u> is <u>cold</u> because of <u>Mr Brocklehurst</u> and cruel teachers.

3) In <u>contrast</u>, there's a "<u>good fire</u>" in <u>Miss Temple's</u> room, a "<u>cheerful fire</u>" in <u>Mrs Fairfax's</u> room and a "<u>glowing</u> peat fire" at <u>Moor House</u> — these are all places where Jane is <u>welcomed</u>.

4) In the <u>fortune-teller</u> scene, Jane says that the usually <u>homely</u> fire "<u>scorches</u>" her. This hints at the <u>pain</u> Mr Rochester will cause her — like being close to the fire, being <u>emotionally</u> close to him will be <u>harmful</u>.

5) The real <u>danger</u> of fire is shown at Thornfield — <u>Bertha</u> almost <u>kills</u> Mr Rochester by setting his <u>bed</u> on <u>fire</u>, and later <u>burns down</u> the entire house. However, it's this fire that <u>allows</u> Mr Rochester and Jane to be <u>together</u> — in this way, fire also symbolises <u>new beginnings</u>.

The red-room symbolises entrapment

1) Jane is sent to the <u>red-room</u> by <u>Mrs Reed</u> as a <u>punishment</u> for fighting with John. Jane is <u>desperate</u> to get out, representing her <u>desire</u> for <u>freedom</u> from the <u>Reeds</u> and her desire for freedom as an <u>individual</u>.

2) The night before Jane leaves Thornfield, she <u>dreams</u> that she's back in the <u>red-room</u>. At this point she feels <u>trapped</u> by <u>Bertha's</u> existence, so she has decided to <u>leave</u> Mr Rochester.

3) It's only <u>after</u> leaving Mr Rochester and Thornfield that Jane experiences <u>freedom</u>. She becomes <u>financially independent</u>, and when she returns to Mr Rochester they are able to marry on <u>equal terms</u>.

Bertha can be seen as a symbol

1) Bertha could <u>symbolise</u> a <u>19th-century wife</u>, who was usually expected to <u>stay</u> at <u>home</u> and look after the house and children. Bertha's <u>madness</u> could symbolise these wives' <u>frustration</u> at their <u>situations</u>.

2) <u>Brontë</u> takes this idea to the <u>extreme</u> by having Bertha <u>locked</u> away and <u>guarded</u> by her husband's employee, Grace Poole.

3) Bertha could also <u>symbolise</u> Jane's <u>desire</u> to <u>rebel</u> — <u>Jane</u> rebels against the <u>restrictions</u> of <u>social conventions</u> just as <u>Bertha</u> rebels against being trapped in her room. Jane tells Mr Rochester "I am <u>no bird</u>; and <u>no net enslaves</u> me" — she is not prepared to be controlled by Mr Rochester.

> **Writer's Techniques**
>
> It's significant that it's <u>Bertha</u> who <u>destroys Thornfield</u>. For her, it represents <u>imprisonment</u> and <u>male domination</u>. In this dramatic last act, she <u>frees herself</u> and she also frees <u>Jane</u>.

"Don't keep me long; the fire scorches me."

Brontë uses fire to symbolise different things — on one hand it represents warmth and the feeling of home, but on the other hand it represents danger and destruction. I think I'll stick to radiators in my house...

Genre

Most books settle for one genre, but *Jane Eyre* is so awesome that there are several genres going on.

'Jane Eyre' has elements of a Gothic novel

1) Gothic novels were <u>popular</u> in the <u>19th century</u> — they generally featured a <u>mysterious location</u>, <u>supernatural</u> elements and disturbing <u>secrets</u>.

2) <u>Thornfield</u> has some Gothic features — its "<u>battlements</u>" make it sound like a <u>castle</u>, and the <u>strange laughs</u> and <u>noises</u> that Jane hears make it seem <u>haunted</u>.

3) <u>Bertha</u> reminds Jane of a "<u>vampire</u>" when she appears in her bedroom. Vampires were <u>common</u> elements of <u>Gothic fiction</u> and the reader wonders what kind of <u>monster</u> is <u>hiding</u> at Thornfield — especially after it "<u>bit</u>" Mr Mason and "sucked the blood".

4) However, the Gothic elements are destroyed towards the end of the novel — the Gothic <u>location</u>, Thornfield, has been <u>burnt down</u> and the Gothic <u>character</u>, Bertha, has <u>died</u>.

It can also be described as a bildungsroman...

1) A <u>bildungsroman</u> is a book where the <u>main character</u> goes on a <u>journey</u> of <u>self-discovery</u> and undergoes significant personal and moral <u>development</u>. In some ways, this is an <u>ideal genre</u> to describe *Jane Eyre*:

- Jane <u>matures</u> and learns to keep her <u>temper</u> and <u>passions</u> under <u>control</u>.
- She <u>overcomes</u> the <u>death</u> of a <u>friend</u>, a <u>failed wedding</u> and a <u>near-death</u> experience.
- She is involved in a <u>search</u> for <u>belonging</u> and a <u>struggle</u> to be with the <u>man</u> she <u>loves</u>.

2) Jane is very <u>self-aware</u> from early on in the novel, which is <u>unusual</u> for a bildungsroman where the protagonist normally learns to understand their character. However, what Jane does is learn to <u>overcome</u> her <u>flaws</u>.

...but you can't ignore the romance

1) A <u>romance</u> is a story that focuses on <u>romantic love</u>. There's usually a <u>happy ending</u> for 'good' characters.

2) Lots of *Jane Eyre* is about <u>Jane</u> and <u>Mr Rochester's</u> <u>relationship</u> — it's a <u>crucial</u> part of the story.

3) There's a sense that they're <u>destined</u> to be together. Although it takes <u>time</u> for the relationship to <u>develop</u>, the reader <u>guesses</u> that it will happen.

4) However, their relationship <u>isn't conventional</u> — they're from <u>different classes</u> and neither is very <u>attractive</u>. Jane requires <u>equality</u> in their relationship, which was an <u>unusual attitude</u> for a <u>woman</u> at the time.

5) It seems that the <u>romance</u> element has <u>disappeared</u> when Jane thinks about marrying <u>St. John</u>, who she doesn't love. But the <u>ending</u> is undoubtedly <u>romantic</u> — Jane <u>gets her man</u> and they <u>live happily ever after</u>.

Look at the mixture of genres Brontë uses in 'Jane Eyre'...

EXAM TIP

The mixture of genres in the novel is a bit like Jane's character — she's a mixture of passion, reason and morality. Oh, and make sure you can spell 'bildungsroman' — or the examiner won't be all that impressed.

Language

I think we should all appreciate Brontë's decision to use language — not sure the book would work otherwise.

The writing style is complex

1) Even as a <u>child</u>, Jane's <u>language</u> is <u>detailed</u> and <u>complex</u> — phrases like "the <u>audible</u> conclusion of my <u>musings</u>" <u>remind</u> the reader that she's writing as an <u>adult looking back</u>.

2) Her sentences are often <u>long</u> and <u>passionate</u> — they can sometimes be <u>difficult</u> to <u>follow</u>, but they allow the reader to <u>understand</u> everything that Jane <u>feels</u> and <u>experiences</u>.

3) Jane <u>doesn't avoid</u> describing <u>difficult moments</u> — she doesn't <u>skip</u> over her <u>heartbreak</u>, and describes how her "wishes" were "<u>corpses</u> that could never revive", after she finds out about <u>Bertha</u>.

Brontë uses detailed descriptions

1) Brontë uses lots of <u>descriptive language</u> to help the reader <u>vividly imagine</u> unusual characters like <u>Bertha</u>: "the <u>clothed hyena</u> rose up, and stood tall on its <u>hind-feet</u>."

2) The descriptions help the reader to <u>visualise</u> and <u>understand</u> Jane's <u>experiences</u>. She describes a scene on the moors with the "stream... catching <u>golden gleams</u> from the sun" — this is a <u>beautiful place</u> which Jane clearly <u>loves</u>.

3) Brontë frequently uses <u>pathetic fallacy</u> — giving <u>human emotions</u> to <u>nature</u> or <u>objects</u>. In particular, Brontë uses the <u>weather</u> to emphasise a character's <u>emotions</u>:

- Jane's <u>optimism</u> when she first arrives at <u>Thornfield</u> is reflected in the <u>bright sunshine</u> that fills her room — "The chamber looked such a <u>bright</u> little place to me as the <u>sun shone in</u>".

- There is a <u>dramatic storm</u> on the night Mr Rochester <u>proposes</u> — "the <u>thunder crashed</u>" and "the <u>lightning gleamed</u>". This mirrors Jane's <u>excitement</u> about her <u>engagement</u>.

Jane's speech is direct but reserved

1) There's a <u>contrast</u> between the <u>detail</u> of Jane's <u>narration</u> and the <u>plainness</u> of her <u>speech</u>. This means that the <u>reader</u> knows much <u>more</u> about her than any of the other <u>characters</u> do.

2) <u>Mr Rochester</u> likes the <u>frankness</u> of Jane's speech — she <u>doesn't</u> try to <u>flatter</u> him, but just <u>speaks</u> her <u>mind</u>.

3) Although Jane's speech is usually <u>measured</u>, sometimes it's very <u>passionate</u>. When Rochester <u>teases</u> her before <u>proposing</u>, she says "Do you think... I am <u>soulless</u> and heartless? <u>You think wrong!</u>"

4) When Jane <u>directly addresses</u> the <u>reader</u>, she uses <u>simpler language</u>, helping them to feel <u>closer</u> to her — "Gentle reader, may you never feel what I then felt!"

Write about how Brontë paints a full picture for the reader...

Brontë is keen for the reader to picture the setting clearly, and to understand exactly what Jane sees and feels. The descriptions are often detailed and can also reflect the mood of the scene. Marvellous.

Practice Questions

The end of the chapter is in sight, but we've just managed to squeeze in some practice questions for you to have a crack at. I know they're not the most exciting part of the book, but sadly not every page can be as downright hilarious as the cartoon at the back (well, I think it's funny...). Go on, give 'em a go — it'd be rude not to...

Quick Questions

1) What is the subtitle of *Jane Eyre*?

2) What is the cliffhanger that Brontë uses at the end of Volume One?

3) How many years does the novel skip while Jane is at Lowood?

4) What does Adèle Varens' dialogue show about her character?

5) Name the five main settings in *Jane Eyre*.

6) Who is Jane with when she says that the fire "scorches" her?

7) Where is the "red-room"? What does it symbolise?

8) Write down the names of three possible genres you could use to describe the novel.

9) Which genre does the ending of *Jane Eyre* feel like it belongs to?

10) Give three reasons why Brontë uses detailed descriptions.

Practice Questions

Time to dive into some deeper questions — these ones will need a bit more thought and you should be aiming to write a paragraph for each of them. Go well, my friend, go well...

In-depth Questions

1) Explain why you think Brontë gets an innkeeper to describe what happened to Thornfield Hall.

2) Do you think that Jane is a reliable narrator? Explain why / why not.

3) How does education help to structure the novel?

4) How does Brontë's use of foreshadowing help to structure *Jane Eyre*?

5) Explain why Jane's journeys are significant in the novel.

6) Why do you think that Jane dreams about the red-room on the night before she leaves Thornfield?

7) Write a paragraph on how Bertha can be seen as a symbol in the novel.

8) Find an example in the text of a detailed description.
   Explain why you think Brontë uses it at that point in the novel.

9) What is 'pathetic fallacy'? How does Brontë use it in the novel?

Practice Questions

Picture the scene — you're sat in a draughty hall, on a blooming uncomfortable chair, and a nasty-looking question booklet has just been plonked on your desk. It's not pretty, but as you flick to the question on 'Jane Eyre', the hint of a smile appears on your face — you've met plenty of pesky questions like this one, and you're ready for it. You pick up your pen, and begin the journey towards GCSE glory...

... sorry, got a bit carried away there. Here are some exam-style questions for you to have a go at:

Exam-style Questions

1) Read this passage from the beginning of Volume One, Chapter 11:

> A new chapter in a novel is something like a new scene in a play, and when I draw up the curtain this time, reader, you must fancy you see a room in the George Inn at Millcote, with such large-figured papering on the walls as inn rooms have: such a carpet, such furniture, such ornaments on the mantel-piece, such prints; including a portrait of George the Third, and another of the Prince of Wales, and a representation of the death of Wolfe. All this is visible to you by the light of an oil-lamp hanging from the ceiling, and by that of an excellent fire, near which I sit in my cloak and bonnet; my muff and umbrella lie on the table, and I am warming away the numbness and chill contracted by sixteen hours' exposure to the rawness of an October day — I left Lowton at four o'clock a.m., and the Millcote town clock is now just striking eight.
>
> Reader, though I look comfortably accommodated, I am not very tranquil in my mind — I thought when the coach stopped here there would be someone to meet me; I looked anxiously round as I descended the wooden steps in the "boots" placed for my convenience, expecting to hear my name pronounced and to see some description of carriage waiting to convey me to Thornfield.

Using this passage as a starting point, write about Jane's role as a narrator.
Write about:
a) the way that Jane acknowledges her role as narrator in this passage
b) the reliability of Jane as a narrator in the novel as a whole

2) How does Brontë use dialogue to show the development of characters and relationships in the novel?

3) Describe the significance of Brontë's use of symbolism in *Jane Eyre*.

4) 'It is impossible to describe *Jane Eyre* using just one genre.'
How far do you agree with this view? Give examples from the novel to support your answer.

Exam Preparation

Getting to know the text will put you at a massive advantage in the exam. It's not enough just to read it though — you've got to get to grips with the nitty-gritty bits. It's all about gathering evidence...

The exam questions will test four main skills

You will need to show the examiner that you can:

1) Write about the text in a <u>thoughtful way</u> — <u>picking out</u> appropriate <u>examples</u> and <u>quotations</u> to back up your opinions.

2) <u>Identify</u> and <u>explain</u> features of the text's <u>form</u>, <u>structure</u> and <u>language</u>. Show how the author uses these to create <u>meanings</u> and <u>effects</u>.

3) Relate the text to its <u>cultural, social and historical background</u>.

4) Write in a <u>clear</u>, <u>well-structured</u> way. <u>5%</u> of the marks in your English Literature exams are for <u>spelling</u>, <u>punctuation</u> and <u>grammar</u>. Make sure that your writing is as <u>accurate</u> as possible.

Preparation is important

1) It's <u>important</u> to cover <u>all</u> the <u>different sections</u> of this book in your <u>revision</u>. You need to make sure you <u>understand</u> the text's <u>context</u>, <u>plot</u>, <u>characters</u>, <u>themes</u> and <u>writer's techniques</u>.

2) In the <u>exam</u>, you'll need to <u>bring together</u> your <u>ideas</u> about these topics to answer the question <u>quickly</u>.

3) Think about the different <u>characters</u> and <u>themes</u> in the text, and write down some <u>key points</u> and <u>ideas</u> about each one. Then, find some <u>evidence</u> to support each point — this could be something from <u>any</u> of the <u>sections</u> in this book. You could set out your evidence in a <u>table</u> like this:

Theme: Gender	
19th-century attitudes	Women sometimes seen as inferior to men, and reliant on husbands. Brontë challenges this — Jane strives for equality.
Oppression of Bertha	Bertha locked away, silenced (has no voice in the novel) and abandoned by society.
Jane's language	Jane speaks frankly and honestly to men as equals — ignores what the social conventions expect.
Unconventional women	Jane — intelligent, independent, strong woman — compare with Miss Oliver. Bertha — "intemperate and unchaste".
Masculinity	Mr Rochester has "stern", masculine appearance, but relies on Jane for moral advice and support. Men try to control Jane.

Preparing to succeed — a cunning plot indeed...

Knowing the plot inside out will be unbelievably helpful in the exam. It'll help you to stay calm and make sure you write a brilliant answer that positively glitters with little gems of evidence. The exam's just a chance for you to show off...

The Exam Question

This page deals with how to approach an exam question. The stuff below will help you get started on a scorching exam answer, more scorching than, say, a phoenix cooking fiery fajitas in a flaming furnace.

Read the question carefully and underline key words

Henry didn't read the weather report carefully enough when planning his weekend activities.

1) The style of question you'll get depends on which <u>exam board</u> you're taking.

2) Read all the <u>instructions</u> carefully. Make sure you know <u>how many</u> questions you need to answer and <u>how much time</u> you should spend answering each one.

3) If the question has <u>more than one part</u>, look at the total number of marks for each bit. This should help you to plan your <u>time</u> in the exam.

4) <u>Read</u> the question at least <u>twice</u> so you completely understand it. <u>Underline</u> the key words. If you're given an <u>extract</u>, underline <u>important</u> words or phrases in that too.

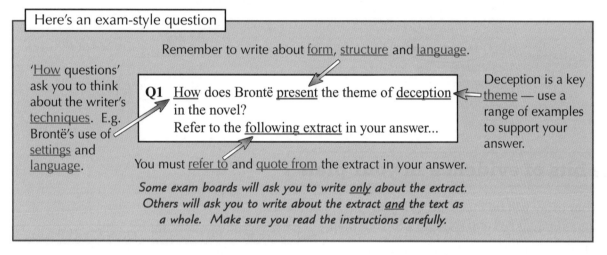

Here's an exam-style question

Remember to write about <u>form</u>, <u>structure</u> and <u>language</u>.

'<u>How</u> questions' ask you to think about the writer's <u>techniques</u>. E.g. Brontë's use of <u>settings</u> and <u>language</u>.

Q1 <u>How</u> does Brontë <u>present</u> the theme of <u>deception</u> in the novel?
Refer to the <u>following extract</u> in your answer...

Deception is a key <u>theme</u> — use a range of examples to support your answer.

You must <u>refer to</u> and <u>quote from</u> the extract in your answer.

Some exam boards will ask you to write <u>only</u> about the extract. Others will ask you to write about the extract <u>and</u> the text as a whole. Make sure you read the instructions carefully.

Get to know exam language

Some <u>words</u> come up time and again in <u>exam questions</u>. Have a look at some <u>specimen</u> questions, pick out words that are <u>often used</u> in questions and make sure that you <u>understand</u> what they mean. You could <u>write a few down</u> whilst you're revising. For example:

Question Word	You need to...
Explore / Explain	Show <u>how</u> the writer deals with a <u>theme</u>, <u>character</u> or <u>idea</u>. Make several <u>different</u> points to answer the question.
How does	Think about the <u>techniques</u> or <u>literary features</u> that the author uses to get their point across.
Give examples	Use <u>direct quotes</u> and describe <u>events</u> from the text in your own words.
Refer to	Read the question so that you know if you need to write about just an <u>extract</u>, or an extract and the <u>rest of the text</u>.

The advice squad — the best cops in the NYPD...

Whatever question you're asked in the exam, your answer should touch on the main characters, themes, structure and language of the text. All the stuff we've covered in the rest of the book in fact. It's so neat, it's almost like we planned it.

Planning Your Answer

I'll say this once — and then I'll probably repeat it several times — it is absolutely, completely, totally and utterly essential that you make a plan before you start writing. Only a fool jumps right in without a plan...

Plan your answer before you start

1) If you plan, you're less likely to forget something <u>important</u>.

2) A good plan will help you <u>organise</u> your ideas — and write a good, <u>well-structured</u> essay.

3) Write your plan at the <u>top of your answer booklet</u> and draw a <u>neat line</u> through it when you've finished.

4) <u>Don't</u> spend <u>too long</u> on your plan. It's only <u>rough work</u>, so you don't need to write in full sentences. Here are a few <u>examples</u> of different ways you can plan your answer:

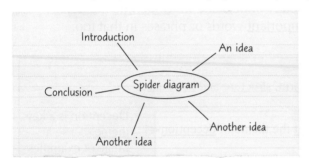

Include bits of evidence in your plan

1) <u>Writing</u> your essay will be much <u>easier</u> if you include <u>important quotes</u> and <u>examples</u> in your plan.

2) You could include them in a <u>table</u> like this one:

3) <u>Don't</u> spend <u>too long</u> writing out quotes though. It's just to make sure you <u>don't forget</u> anything when you write your answer.

A point...	Quote to back this up...
Another point...	Quote...
A different point...	Example...
A brand new point...	Quote...

Structure your answer

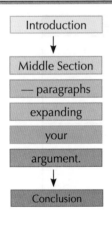

1) Your <u>introduction</u> should give a brief answer to the question you're writing about. Make it clear how you're going to <u>tackle the topic</u>.

2) The <u>middle section</u> of your essay should explain your answer in detail and give evidence to back it up. Write a <u>paragraph</u> for each point you make. Make sure you <u>comment</u> on your evidence and <u>explain how</u> it helps to <u>prove</u> your point.

3) Remember to write a <u>conclusion</u> — a paragraph at the end which <u>sums up</u> your <u>main points</u>. There's <u>more</u> about introductions and conclusions on the <u>next page</u>.

Dirk finally felt ready to tackle the topic.

To plan or not to plan, that is the question...

The answer is yes, yes, a thousand times yes. Often students dive right in, worried that planning will take up valuable time. But 5 minutes spent organising a well-structured answer is loads better than pages of waffle. Mmm waffles.

Writing Introductions and Conclusions

Now you've made that plan that I was banging on about on the last page, you'll know what your main points are. This is going to make writing your introduction and conclusion as easy as pie.

Get to the point straight away in your introduction

1) First, you need to <u>work out</u> what the question is <u>asking you</u> to do:

> How is the character of St. John Rivers important to the novel?

> The question is <u>asking you</u> to think about the <u>role</u> of <u>St. John Rivers</u> in the text.
> Plan your essay by thinking about <u>how</u> St. John Rivers <u>links</u> to the novel's <u>plot</u> and <u>themes</u>.

2) When you've <u>planned</u> your essay, you should <u>begin</u> by giving a <u>clear answer</u> to the <u>question</u> in a sentence or two. Use the <u>rest</u> of the <u>introduction</u> to <u>develop</u> this idea. Try to include the <u>main paragraph ideas</u> that you have listed in your plan, but <u>save</u> the <u>evidence</u> for later.

3) You could also use the <u>introduction</u> to give your <u>opinion</u>. Whatever you do, make sure your introduction makes it <u>clear</u> how your answer <u>fits the question</u>.

Your conclusion must answer the question

1) The <u>most important</u> thing you have to do at the <u>end</u> of your writing is to <u>summarise</u> your <u>answer</u> to the question.

2) It's your <u>last chance</u> to persuade the examiner, so make your <u>main point</u> again.

3) Use your <u>last sentence</u> to really <u>impress</u> the <u>examiner</u> — it will make your essay finish in an <u>impressive way</u>. You could <u>develop</u> your own <u>opinion</u> of the text or <u>highlight</u> which of your <u>points</u> you thought was the most <u>interesting</u>.

The examiner was struggling to see the answer clearly.

Use the question words in your introduction and conclusion

1) Try to use <u>words</u> or <u>phrases</u> from the <u>question</u> in your introduction and conclusion.

> How does Brontë use setting in the novel?

2) This will show the examiner that you're <u>answering the question</u>.

> Brontë uses setting in 'Jane Eyre' to create symbolic meaning. The different settings each reflect something about the characters who live there.

The first line of the introduction gives a clear answer, which will lead on to the rest of the essay.

3) This will also help you keep the question <u>fresh in your mind</u> so your answer doesn't <u>wander off-topic</u>.

I've come to the conclusion that I really like pie...

To conclude, the introduction eases the examiner in gently, whilst the conclusion is your last chance to impress. But remember — the examiner doesn't want to see any new points lurking in those closing sentences.

Writing Main Paragraphs

So we've covered the beginning and the end, now it's time for the meaty bit. The roast beef in between the prawn cocktail and the treacle tart. This page is about how to structure your paragraphs. It's quite simple...

P.E.E.D. is how to put your argument together

Remember to start a new paragraph every time you make a new point.

1) P.E.E.D. stands for: Point, Example, Explain, Develop.

2) Begin each paragraph by making a point. Then give an example from the text (either a quote or a description). Next, explain how your example backs up your point.

3) Finally, try to develop your point by writing about its effect on the reader, how it links to another part of the text or what the writer's intention is in including it.

Use short quotes to support your ideas

1) Don't just use words from the novel to show what happens in the plot...

> Miss Temple is kind — "not the least delight of the entertainment was the smile of gratification with which our hostess regarded us".

This just gives an example from the text without offering any explanation or analysis.

2) Instead, it's much better to use short quotes as evidence to support a point you're making.

3) It makes the essay structure more fluent and focused if most quotes are embedded in your sentences.

> Miss Temple is kind to Jane at Lowood — she gives some "seed-cake" to Jane and Helen Burns when they are in her room. This contrasts with the awful food that the girls are normally given at the school...

It's better to use short, embedded quotes as evidence. Then you can go on to explain them.

Get to know some literary language

1) Using literary terms in your answer will help you get top marks — as long as you use them correctly.

2) When you're revising, think about literary terms that are relevant to the text and how you might include them in an essay. Take a look at the table below for some examples.

Literary Term	Definition	Example
Foreshadowing	When the author hints at a future event.	"Your bride stands between us."
Pathetic fallacy	Giving human emotions to aspects of nature or objects.	"Nature must be gladsome when I was so happy."
Symbol	Something used by an author to represent something else.	Fire symbolises danger: "the fire scorches me."

This page is so exciting — I nearly...

Now now, let's all be grown-ups and avoid the obvious joke. It's a good way of remembering how to structure your paragraphs though. Point, Example, Explain, Develop. Simple. Maybe we could make a rap or something... anyone?

In the Exam

Keeping cool in the exam can be tricky. But if you take in all the stuff on this page, you'll soon have it down to a fine art. Then you can stroll out of that exam hall with the swagger of an essay-writing master.

Don't panic if you make a mistake

1) Okay, so say you've timed the exam beautifully. Instead of putting your feet up on the desk for the last 5 minutes, it's a good idea to <u>read through</u> your <u>answers</u> and <u>correct any mistakes</u>...

2) If you want to get rid of a mistake, <u>cross it out</u>. <u>Don't scribble</u> it out as this can look messy. Make any corrections <u>neatly</u> and <u>clearly</u> instead of writing on top of the words you've already written.

> techniques
> The author uses various literary ~~teknikues~~ to explore this theme.

This is the clearest way to correct a mistake. Don't be tempted to try writing on top of the original word.

3) If you've <u>left out</u> a <u>word</u> or a <u>phrase</u> and you've got space to add it in <u>above</u> the line it's missing from, write the missing bit above the line with a '^' to show exactly where it should go.

Re-read the sentence carefully to work out where the '^' symbol needs to go.

> and hyperbole
> The writer uses imagery to draw attention to this point.

4) If you've left out whole <u>sentences</u> or <u>paragraphs</u>, write them in a <u>separate section</u> at the <u>end</u> of the essay. Put a <u>star</u> (*) next to both the <u>extra writing</u> and the <u>place</u> you want it to go.

Always keep an eye on the time

1) It's surprisingly <u>easy</u> to <u>run out of time</u> in exams. You've got to leave <u>enough time</u> to answer <u>all</u> the questions you're asked to do. You've also got to leave enough time to <u>finish</u> each essay properly — with a <u>clear ending</u>.

2) Here are some <u>tips</u> on how to <u>avoid</u> running out of time:

- Work out <u>how much time</u> you have for each part of your answer <u>before</u> you <u>start</u>.

- Take off a few minutes at the beginning to <u>plan</u>, and a <u>few minutes</u> at the end for your <u>conclusion</u>.

- Make sure you have a <u>watch</u> to <u>time yourself</u> — and keep checking it.

- Be <u>strict</u> with yourself — if you spend <u>too long</u> on one part of your answer, you may run out of time.

- If you're <u>running out of time</u>, keep <u>calm</u>, <u>finish</u> the <u>point</u> you're on and move on to your <u>conclusion</u>.

Stephanie never had a problem with keeping cool.

Treat an exam like a spa day — just relax...

Some people actually do lose the plot when they get into the exam. The trick is to keep calm and well... carry on. If you make sure you get your exam technique sorted, you'll be as relaxed as a sloth in a room full of easy chairs.

Sample Exam Question

And now the bit you've all been waiting for — a sample exam question and a lovely little plan.
Go and make yourself a cup of tea, then settle down and enjoy.

Here's a sample exam question...

Read this feisty exam question. That's the best way to start...

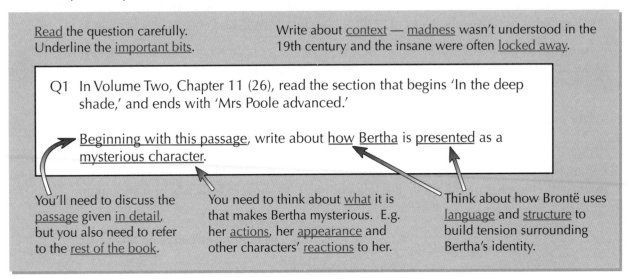

Read the question carefully.
Underline the important bits.

Write about context — madness wasn't understood in the 19th century and the insane were often locked away.

> Q1 In Volume Two, Chapter 11 (26), read the section that begins 'In the deep shade,' and ends with 'Mrs Poole advanced.'
>
> Beginning with this passage, write about how Bertha is presented as a mysterious character.

You'll need to discuss the passage given in detail, but you also need to refer to the rest of the book.

You need to think about what it is that makes Bertha mysterious. E.g. her actions, her appearance and other characters' reactions to her.

Think about how Brontë uses language and structure to build tension surrounding Bertha's identity.

Here's how you could plan your answer

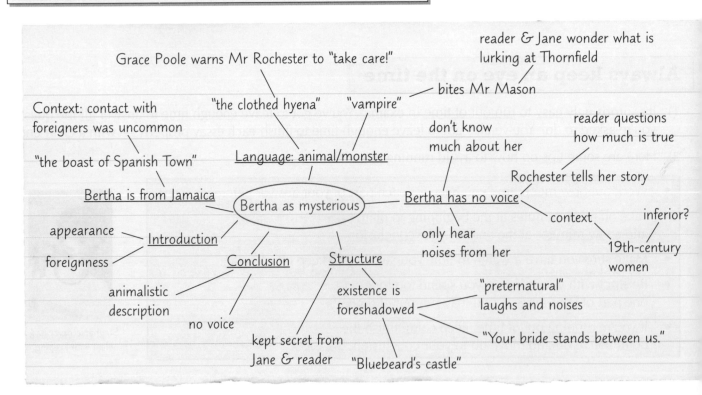

What do examiners eat? Why, egg-sam-wiches of course...

The most important thing to remember is DON'T PANIC. Take a deep breath, read the question, read it again, write a plan... take another deep breath... and start writing. Leave 5 minutes at the end to check your answer too.

Worked Answer

These pages will show you how to take an OK answer and turn it into a really good one that will impress the examiner.

Use your introduction to get off to a good start

These pages are all about how to word your sentences to impress the examiner, so we haven't included everything from the plan on page 70.

You might start with something like...

> Bertha is presented as a mysterious character in a number of ways, including her foreignness and appearance. Also, Bertha never speaks, so the reader knows very little about her.

1) This intro is <u>okay</u>. It acknowledges that Bertha is mysterious for <u>different reasons</u>.
2) It's also a good idea to use the <u>key words</u> in the question to give your essay <u>focus</u> and show the examiner you're on <u>track</u> and that you're thinking about the question from the start.
3) But there's still room for <u>improvement</u>...

This intro talks about the social and historical context.

> Brontë uses a number of different techniques to present Bertha as a mysterious character: she is described in animalistic terms; she does not speak; and she is a foreigner — meaning that she was an outsider in early 19th century society. This is reinforced by the way she is locked away at Thornfield. Neither the reader nor Jane knows of Bertha's existence until the end of Volume Two, but her presence is foreshadowed by a series of unexplained and mysterious events.

This tells the examiner what the essay's about and shows that you've thought about your essay structure.

Develop each point with detailed comments and quotes

> Jane describes Bertha using animal-related vocabulary when she goes up to her room. The combination of descriptions create a grotesque picture, and Bertha screams rather than speaking.

1) This paragraph makes several different <u>points</u> about Jane's reaction to Bertha. But it doesn't <u>develop</u> the points <u>fully</u> by giving quotes or talking about the language used.
2) You should develop your points with <u>detail</u> and comments on the effect on the reader:

This makes a relevant point about the extract, and then goes on to give more detail.

> Jane's description of Bertha's physical appearance when Mr Rochester takes her to see Bertha adds to the mystery. Jane describes Bertha as if she is an animal, and at first she cannot even tell if Bertha is a "beast or human being". Brontë builds up a grotesque picture using animalistic vocabulary. Bertha stands on her "hind-feet" and has hair that is "wild as a mane" — the reader is given lots of description, which makes her sound inhuman, creating a sense that she is threatening and powerful. Jane also mentions Bertha's "purple face" which she first saw when Bertha appeared in Jane's bedroom. Jane thought that Bertha was a "vampire" and even though Bertha has now been revealed as a human, she maintains an air of mystery, and the reader is left with many questions about her character.

Analysing Brontë's use of language will help you get top marks.

This shows that you've thought about other parts of the book, not just the passage given in the question.

Remember to back up your points with quotes from the novel.

Worked Answer

You need to make a variety of points

Here's a point you could make about the way that Bertha is described in this extract:

> Brontë adds to the mystery surrounding Bertha by not giving her a voice. Instead, she is heard giving a "fierce cry" and Grace Poole answers for her when Mr Rochester asks how Bertha is doing.

1) This paragraph builds on the idea that Bertha is mysterious because she's not given a voice.
2) However, you can improve it by discussing how this relates to the themes of the novel:

> Bertha doesn't speak when Jane and the others are in her room, adding to the mystery surrounding her. Instead, she lets out a "fierce cry" and gazes "wildly" at the people around her — this animalistic imagery confirms that Bertha is mad. The fact that Bertha has no voice in the novel links to the wider theme of gender. Women in the novel are often controlled or manipulated by men. For example, Jane is bullied by John Reed and Mr Brocklehurst, and Mr Rochester manipulates Blanche Ingram. Jane rebels against this and achieves equality with Mr Rochester, but Bertha only rebels wordlessly, through violence, which maintains the mystery surrounding her.

It's a good idea to show the examiner you're aware of how the extract displays the themes of the novel.

Don't forget to explain how your points link to the exam question.

3) You could develop this by focussing on the context in which the novel was written:

The examiner will be impressed if you can link the extract to the context at the time the novel was written.

> Women in the 19th century were considered to be inferior to men in some ways, and Bertha could be seen as a symbol for women who didn't have jobs or much of a voice in society. The fact that Bertha has no voice in the novel reflects the status of women at the time, who often felt oppressed by men.

Finish your essay in style

You could say:

> In conclusion, this extract shows that Bertha is a mysterious character through animalistic descriptions of her appearance and behaviour as well as the fact that she does not speak.

1) This conclusion is okay, but it doesn't summarise how Brontë makes Bertha seem mysterious.
2) So to make it really impressive you could say something like...

> Bertha is at the heart of the secrets at Thornfield, and she is presented as a mysterious character. Brontë's detailed description of her uses animalistic and monstrous language to create a sense of the unknown, but it is the fact that Bertha never speaks that ensures her mysterious status. The reader never hears Bertha tell her own story, and is therefore left with a strong curiosity about her.

Now's your chance to give your own opinion about which of Brontë's techniques creates the most mystery.

Make your last sentence really stand out — it's your last opportunity to impress the examiner.

Why do alligators write good essays? Their quotes are so snappy...

It seems like there's a lot to remember on these two pages, but there's not really. To summarise — write a scorching intro and a sizzling conclusion, make a good range of points (one per paragraph) and include plenty of examples. Easy.

Index

Index

The Characters in 'Jane Eyre'

Phew! You should be an expert on *Jane Eyre* by now. But if you want a bit of light relief and a quick recap of the novel's plot, sit yourself down and read through *Jane Eyre — The Cartoon*...

Jane Eyre

growing up

as an adult

John Reed

Mrs Reed

Helen Burns

Mrs Fairfax

Adèle Varens

Edward Rochester

Blanche Ingram

Mr Mason

Bertha Mason

St. John Rivers

Diana and Mary Rivers

Charlotte Brontë's 'Jane Eyre'

JANE IS AN ORPHAN WHO LIVES WITH HER NASTY AUNT AND CRUEL COUSINS.

Take that! That'll teach you to read my books!

Oww! I hate you, you big bully!

John Reed

Jane Eyre

Evil girl! How dare you hurt my ickle baby? I'll lock you in the red-room.

Nooo! Not the haunted red-room!

Mrs Reed

IN THE RED-ROOM

Arrgghh! Help!

A FEW MONTHS LATER, MRS REED FINDS A WAY TO GET RID OF JANE

Right, you're off to boarding school.

Hooray! I hate it here... and I hate you, you old bag.

Gasp I've told Mr Brocklehurst, the master, what a liar you are, so expect beatings.

AT LOWOOD SCHOOL...

Blimey, school's tough. I'm cold and hungry, and some teachers are mean.

Hi, I'm Helen, *cough*. The teachers only beat us for our own good.

Hmmm.

Helen Burns

MR BROCKLEHURST VISITS

Liar, liar, pants on fire! Stand on that stool for the day...

...and you lot, stop looking so pretty.

Mr Brocklehurst

LATER, IN MISS TEMPLE'S ROOM

I'm not a liar, *sob*.

I believe you, Jane.

Miss Temple

cough

Something's not right with Helen. I just can't put my finger on it...

THERE'S A TYPHUS OUTBREAK

Sorry, Jane, Helen's dead — though strangely not of typhus.

Nooooo!

Ofsted won't like all these deaths...

8 YEARS LATER...

I want some adventure, some glamour, some risk. I'm going to be... a governess.

Jane Eyre

JANE ARRIVES AT THORNFIELD

Welcome dear, I'm the housekeeper. The master's away, but here's his ward — she's your pupil. She's French!

Mrs Fairfax

Ooh la la!

Adèle

THE NEXT DAY...

Ahahaha!

Did you hear that mad laughter?

That'll be Grace Poole, our resident weirdo... just ignore her.

3 MONTHS LATER, JANE HELPS A MAN WHO'S FALLEN OFF HIS HORSE

You bewitched my horse!

Mr Rochester

Um... sorry?

BACK AT THORNFIELD, JANE IS SUMMONED BY MR ROCHESTER

Aha, so this ugly mug is my boss.

Tell me your story — unless it's long.

Went to school, came here.

Apparently not.

JANE HEARS A STRANGE NOISE IN THE NIGHT...

Oi, wake up!

Eek, fire! I mean, ahem, *manly noise*.

I heard that weird laugh again...

Ssh! Don't tell anyone. Thanks for saving my life.

Any time, snuggums. *sigh*

TWO WEEKS LATER...

I wish Mr R hadn't gone away...

Oooh, a letter from Mr R — he's bringing all his posh friends here. One of the ladies is gorgeous... and single! He'll probably marry her!

Gasp

I'll flirt with Blanche and see if Jane gets jealous.

Ugh! Governesses are such morons. Ha ha!

Bonjour!

Children are such a drag — send her to school!

Blanche Ingram

What a cow... Edward deserves better.

A FORTUNE-TELLER VISITS...

Mr R's not very rich...

Eww. I'm not marrying a pauper.

Admit it, you're in luuurve with Mr R!

Gasp! How did you — Hang on, you look familiar... Mr R?!

Busted.

THERE'S A VISITOR...

Surprise! Remember me, mate?

Uh oh...!

Mr Mason

ETJE41